Richard H. Horne

Laura Dibalzo

The Patriot Martyrs

Richard H. Horne

Laura Dibalzo
The Patriot Martyrs

ISBN/EAN: 9783337307066

Printed in Europe, USA, Canada, Australia, Japan

Cover: Foto ©Thomas Meinert / pixelio.de

More available books at **www.hansebooks.com**

LAURA DIBALZO

OR

THE PATRIOT MARTYRS

A Tragedy

BY

RICHARD HENGIST HORNE

London:

NEWMAN & CO.
43, OXFORD STREET.

1880.

DRYDEN PRESS:
J. DAVY AND SONS, 137, LONG ACRE, LONDON.

Dedicated

TO

The Illustrious Memory of

WASHINGTON

AND

To the equally pure Patriotic Names of

KOSCIUSKO

KOSSUTH

MAZZINI

AND

GARIBALDI

PREFACE.

WHATEVER the reader may think of the acts and words of the leading characters in this Tragedy, there is nothing set down which the history of the Neapolitan Government of that period does not fully and literally declare and corroborate, whether in atrocious cruelties or heroic fortitude of resistance.

These scenes were written, for the most part, during the lifetime of JOSEPH MAZZINI, from whom I derived much information; availing myself also of what is contained in his published writings, and in the narratives of SILVIO PELLICO, BARON CARLO POERIO, and other Italian martyrs to political liberty. Several of my characters are *portraits*, the faithfulness of which will easily be recognized by those readers who are conversant with the history of Naples during the time in question.

I have always highly honoured Mr. GLADSTONE for his two "*Letters to Lord Aberdeen*" (in 1850, &c.), so worthy of the true spirit of an English gentleman and statesman; and I also honour the reading British Public of that day, for the significant and pregnant fact that those forcible exhibitions of, and protests against foreign abominations in despotism, passed through fourteen editions as rapidly as if they had related to immediate and most poignant interests at home.

It will be at once perceived by all students of the high-class tragic drama (however reduced the number may now be) that the present Tragedy, like all my previous dramas, is systematically constructed for stage representation,— a few speeches being, as usual, cut down to square with the imperative "clock;" but until we have a National Theatre, as in Paris, which shall not be, of necessity, a commercial speculation, there is no hope for me, nor can I reasonably expect to live to see so important a national Educator established. "Night must it be ere Friedland's star shall beam." But here— as so long and motley an interlude has occurred since I have offered any new drama to the world — let me record "my full and heightened" sense of the generously unrestrained and unalloyed estimation expressed by contemporaries best qualified to judge on such matters. It was said by Goethe that his tragedies "were written with his blood." I say the same with regard to mine; and, after upwards of forty years of publicity, I think it will be only handsome in the reader to pardon the above remarks.

On the present occasion I desire to tender my thanks to my friend Mr. ROBERT BROWNING, for an important critical premonition, and to Mr. H. BUXTON FORMAN for his kind and valuable revision of the proofs while passing through the press.

In Dedicating these scenes of my only work that can be designated as of direct political bearing, to the names of five of the world's most distinguished Patriots, a regret has lingered in my mind at omitting others, together with a consciousness that one, at least, of those mentioned, has long since passed above and beyond the range of complimentary reference, and taken his fixed place in the constellated histories of great Nations.

R. H. H.

DRAMATIS PERSONÆ.

SALOMBA; King of Naples.
THE MARQUIS RIVEROLA; A Neapolitan Noble.
CLAUDIO DIBALZO; A Sicilian Gentleman.
ISIDORO GUARINI; A Genoese Gentleman.
CAPTAIN MESZLENKI BATTHYMAROS; A Hungarian Exile.
MICHAEL SKURDENKA; A Polish Jew.
LUCA SFORGLIA; Commissario of the Royal Police.
SILVIO PANORIO; a Prisoner in St. Elmo.
PADRE SAN-VOLPE; the King's Confessor.
PECCHENDA; a Lawyer.
STRONGI'TH'ARM STONEWING; an English Gentleman.
CYRILLE; a French Locksmith.
ILARIO; Valet to DIBALZO.
JAILER of the St. Elmo Prison.

LAURA DIBALZO; Wife of DIBALZO, and Sister of GUARINI.
EDITA DIBALZO; her infant Daughter.
VALENTINE; LAURA'S Lady's-maid, Daughter of CYRILLE.

First and Second Nobles of the Court, First and Second Vintagers, Officer of Police, the King's Secretary, Guards, Police, Peasants, Sailors, Populace, Lazzaroni, &c.

The Scene of the Tragedy is Naples and the environs.

LAURA DIBALZO.

ACT I.

SCENE I.—[4th *Entrance.*]

STREET IN NAPLES.—*An ornamental wall runs along the back, above which is seen the upper part of the Palace of the King, but at some distance.—The Scene darkens as the Curtain rises; and a faint flash of lightning is seen, followed by a roll of thunder in the distance.*

Enter SKURDENKA *and* BATTHYMAROS (L.) *followed by* DIBALZO, *who stands apart, thoughtfully.*

BATT. I think you are superstitious.
SKUR. Say, prophetic:
I mean, I read in yonder angry Heaven
A judgment which some day will shed new light
On kneeling patriots' heads and martyrs' graves.
All men are superstitious, in degree,
Who feel the influence of a spiritual world.
BATT. That, one would rather call devoutness.

Skur. Well—
Call it e'en as ye list, to me the voice
Of Heaven seem'd now to speak.

Dibal. (*coming forward*) With javelins pointing
At yonder cursed pile, where dwells our Fate—
That Fate a man, as mortal as ourselves,
And yet we bear it,—but not patiently.

Skur. And that is right, for patience is no virtue
When it outlives all reasonable hope.
Have you no tidings of Panorio?

Dibal. (*gloomily*) None.   [Dibalzo,

Skur. (*to* Batthymaros) A dear friend of the Signor
A scholar, sir, of many high attainments,
Who suddenly disappeared.

Dibal. 'Tis now two months.
I fear Panorio hath become suspected
Of too much love for Italy.

Skur. 'Tis likely.
Is't true that Muratori, the young student,
And Sisto Andreoli, the sculptor—

Dibal. Yes—
Both have been crush'd—I know what you would ask.

Batt. How crush'd? what mean you?

Skur. (*to* Dibalzo) He's not long in Naples—
My friend, sir, Captain Meszlenki Batthymaros,
Late of the Hungarian Patriotic Guard,
Whose blood made red the snows ere Buda fell:
Rough soldier and true gentleman in one.   [this stone

Batt. (*smiling*) Therefore excuse my bluntness. What is
You speak about?

DIBAL. A newly invented death:
(The King's device: the devil has various talents).
A ponderous flat stone sustained in air
By ropes and beams above a prostrate victim,
Is suddenly detach'd—and by its fall
Changes the noblest image on the earth
Into a quivering mass .... the wolfish eyes
Of the most hardened executioners
Cannot look on it when the stone is raised.
Thus died Andreoli and Muratori,
Suspected of the crime of patriotism,
Being members of *La Giovine Italia*,
Or the society of *La Jeune Europe;*
The accusers, as the judges, knew not which,
Nor cared to know: the King desired their death.
Pray heaven Panorio be not in his fangs. [believe

SKUR. (*to* BATT.) You thought me superstitious: do you
Such things can last?

BATT. They should not last an hour. [foreigner,—

DIBAL. (*lowering his voice*) Ah! do you say so! you, a
And we Italians still endure these wrongs!
 [*taking him by the hand and looking round.*
I'd speak with you in some more private place.
(*to* SKURDENKA) You likewise, sir.

SKUR. We have wrongs, deep enough,
And countries dear to memory—Poland and Hungary
Can sympathize with you.

DIBAL. (*looking off* L.) Soft! draw apart—
'Tis dangerous for men to speak together—
It is the King! he comes from mass.

BATT. (*with an incredulous smile*) Indeed!

B 2

Can he affect devotion?
(*to* DIBALZO) Well—present me
As a good Mussulman.

DIBAL. Hush! stand aside.

[*They separate.* SKURDENKA *stands back* (L.), BATTHYMAROS *in front* (R.), *and* DIBALZO *seats himself on an abutment of the wall.*

Enter SFORGLIA (L.) *followed by Officer and Guards with drawn swords. Guards pause;* SFORGLIA *glances round at* DIBALZO, SKURDENKA *and* BATTHYMAROS.

Enter KING SALOMBA (L.) *attended by* PADRE SAN-VOLPE, *the* MARQUIS RIVEROLA, NOBLES, *and Servants.*

KING. That miracle of our most holy Saint
Gennaro, at the which those kneeling throngs
And prostrate devotees but now rejoiced
Our eyes, and comforted our hearts with proof
Of heavenly favour and of popular power,
Methinks was wrought more fully than of yore.
The crusted blood more freely 'gan to melt,
Ferment, and trickle; and it rose—some said so—
Higher within the glass?

SAN-VOL. It did, my liege.

KING. 'Tis well. We look with love and confidence
Tow'rds all the priesthood, that the miracle
Of holy Saint Vincenzo, by whose prayers
The up-drawn ringer of the sacred bell
(As well thou know'st all records testify)
Suspended hung i' the air—shall better work
Than last year's unbless'd rites. Your preparations

Must have more zest. You understand these things.
Let the lord Cardinal be advised of this.
[SAN-VOLPE bows humbly.
Also the annual growth of our Lord's hair
Beneath the veil that o'er his image falls,
Should, with all sanctity—
[*suddenly observing* SKURDENKA, BATTHYMAROS *and* DI-
BALZO (*and turning to* SFORGLIA) Who are these men?
SFOR. I know them all your Majesty; and one
Is newly come.
KING. They have not been to witness
The miracle. Have eye on them.
SFOR. (*bowing*) I shall, sire. [Jews—
KING. We'll have no Greek Church, Protestants, nor
And one of these doth savour of the last.
[*A servant hands a paper privately to* RIVEROLA.
KING. (*catching sight of it*) What's that?
RIVE. (*presenting paper*) Your Majesty, 'tis a petition
From the aged father, with the wife and sister,
Of Sannyro Cittadini, and Pietro—
KING. (*interrupting*) Ah!
I had forgotten. (*to* SFORGLIA) See that they be hung
At sun-down. Stay—or shot (*pauses*), no matter which.
SFOR. With previous torture should they not divulge
The names of their associates—
KING. (*sternly askance*) I thought
You knew your duty, sir! (*devoutly*) as I know mine.
RIVE. My Liege, will you vouchsafe that I remind you
Of Silvio Panorio (DIBALZO *bends forward to listen*) still
[in prison,

Though at his trial proved quite innocent
Of all the charges. 'Twas another man
Of the same name, who wrote the treasonous verse
On the Church wall.

KING. They both wrote verses, then,
It seems.   Where is this other?

RIVE. Fled, my Liege.
But for Panorio—

KING. (*sternly*) "Let him remain
Till the right man be found."
(*to* SAN-VOLPE.) Come, holy father:
While treason scrawls its own doom on the walls,
The Church, and prostrate people are with me.

> [*Exit* KING (R.) *leaning on his* CONFESSOR, *and followed by* SFORGLIA, NOBLES, *Guards and Servants.*

RIVE. (*aside hastily to* DIBALZO.) Keep within doors.
DIBAL. Panorio—
RIVE. You have heard.

> [*Exit hastily* (R.) *after* KING, &c.

(DIBALZO *presses his hand upon his forehead.*)

BATT. (*to* SKURDENKA.) What think you now, my friend, of superstition,
Which can work miracles both ways: for the right,
In spiritual minds,—and for worst wrongs
When grossly put to service?

SKUR. (*fiercely*) Said he not
He'd have no Greek Church, Synagogue, nor Jews?

DIBAL. He did—and said so as he glanced on you.
SKUR. I noted it. A Jew he found in me,
Proud of his race,—though I am not less faithful
To violated Poland.
BATT. Nor will the tyrant
Allow a Protestant Church.
DIBAL. He will allow
No secret conference in a man's own soul,
If he can help it.
BATT. (*half laughing*) But since that's absurd,
Men scorn, and laugh at him.
SKUR. And curse him too.
DIBAL. (*looking around cautiously*) Gentlemen—
I may trust you—I feel sure,
As you may trust me with your patriot thoughts.
I have a noble wife—a child, as dear—
Let them be hostages for my good faith
In this vile city, seeded thick with spies
Nestling 'neath stones, up-shooting in all paths,
Who seek to entangle men in desperate plots
Against the King—in order to betray.
First let me show my confidence in you.
[*looking round on all sides.*
For some time I have sought to organize
An insurrection here. Stand closer. Briefly—
There are some nobles, friends, and gentlemen
Of patriot courage, wealth, and education,
Ready to join me. May I think of you?
Of one—or both? Italian liberty
Strikes not such poignant roots within your hearts

As thoughts of Poland and of Hungary;
But now our struggle is, as was your own—
A sacred resolution of the soul.
    SKUR. We know this—and we feel it.
    BATT. I will join you.
                    [DIBALZO *takes each by the hand.*
    DIBAL. I look you both directly in the eyes—
And see the honour, which I hope you read
In mine as clearly. Gentlemen, farewell!
You shall hear more anon. [*Going* (L.)
    SKUR. We wait your summons.
            [*Exeunt* SKURDENKA *and* BATTHYMAROS (R.)
    DIBAL. Now is a great step taken in the dark,
Which leads to victory, and my country's freedom,
My own fair share of honour in her blessings—
Or else it leads me straightway to the scaffold,
Follow'd perchance by those whom most I love:
My wife—my dearest friends—(*looking off* L.) so, at
Guarini meets me.   [best time

            Enter GUARINI (L.)

    GUAR. (*gravely*) I observed who left you.
    DIBAL. I have entrusted them with my design.
    GUAR. And do they find it wise?
    DIBAL. They never questioned it.
    GUAR. (*impressively*) My friend—my brother—
You know that I am ready to lay down
My life for Italy—placing my head
Beside yours on the scaffold—my last thoughts

Devoted with my heart to our poor country;
My last sigh—gazing up for the last time
At yon blue heaven's impenetrable calm—
Not for myself and my own darkening hour,
But for the doubtful prospect of the cause
For which we die. Pray bear with me a moment.
I think our chances bad, because the people,
Ignorant, priest-poison'd, mass-and-miracle-mad,
Will not support an insurrection through,
But from the vortex at all points fly off,
And fall like sand amidst conflicting winds.
'Twere otherwise in Rome; but here the King
(Amidst a people fierce as lava streams,
But with no Roman souls) is more than Pope.

DIBAL. Yes, he is more of Devil. Oh, Guarini!
Leave your deep thoughts and complex meditations,
Which have so long restrain'd my fix'd resolve:
See how the noblest lives are blotted out
By this one plague-font! Executions, tortures,
Imprisonments through years for trivial acts—
Sometimes for mere suspicion of men's thoughts.
Our friend Panorio, I but now have learnt
Is languishing in chains for an offence
Committed by another of his name!
Can you conceive it?

GUAR. Yes, and bitterly.
Being a man of learning, it was thought
He read the doom of tyrants of all time;
Add but to this the wantonness of power,
And we may understand Salomba gloats,

As though some demon held a saint in chains.
He'll see the heavens no more, until he pass
With white wings through the gates!

[DIBALZO *pauses, then looks off* (L.)

DIBAL. I'll visit him
In his foul dungeon!

GUAR. Have you private means?

DIBAL. I have—I have. See'st yonder man? (L.)

GUAR. I do.

DIBAL. His life I lately saved. He now is jailer
In the state prison. [*Going* (L.)

GUAR. Can you safely trust him?

DIBAL. I can! I must! [*Exit hastily* (L.)

GUAR. I would have bade him think
Of Laura, and her child, had she not been
My sister. But our dearest private feelings
Claim not the foremost rank in times like these.

Enter the MARQUIS RIVEROLA (R.) *with caution.*

RIVE. Guarini, make your brother-in-law aware
He is in danger of the King's suspicion.

GUAR. So, Marquis, are we all.

RIVE. 'Tis greater reason (*looking round*)
That shadowy tree we wot of, should be shaken.

GUAR. Before the fruit's well set.

RIVE. Green though it be,
And doubtful, our delays were certain ruin.

GUAR. (*calmly*) Are we betrayed?

RIVE. I mean not that,—no, no—
But fear the germinations of our thoughts,

Imbedded in the breast of many friends,
Will sing in darkness round the palace walls,
Until they vibrate in Salomba's ear.

   GUAR. This is mere apprehension.

   RIVE. Not entirely.
Sforglia begins to look askance at me,
And of Dibalzo spake but now, as one
Who seem'd to have much business on his mind:
All which I treated casually—scarce heard it—
But we must all be watchful, day and night.

   GUAR. Are we so deep ere the first plunge?

   RIVE. (*impatiently*) You brood
Too much, and all too widely in your views.

   GUAR. My hopes embrace all Italy.

   RIVE. And therefore
Lack concentration. Freedom must begin
At one point first. You seem to believe in nought
But reasoning.

   GUAR. Marquis, you mistake my bent:
For 'tis not wisdom that propels life's wheels,
Retarding rather, by its weight of thoughts;
'Tis noble passions only move the world—
The rest is speculation.

   RIVE. But look round:
See how bad passions move!

   GUAR. Aye—backward, Sir.
I spake of man's good progress.

   RIVE. Say you so?
Then why not act at once?

   GUAR. Because I doubt

The structure and foundation of your plans.

RIVE. We have more friends in secret than you dream—All, save his hirelings.

GUAR. And the priest-led People.

[*after a thoughtful pause.*]
Let us think closely on it—but not here.

[*Exeunt* (L.)]

SCENE II.—[2nd *Entrance.*]

Gloomy passage in the St. Elmo Prison.—Three Dungeon doors along the back, strongly barred across. Prison bell strikes three, in the morning.

Enter JAILER *with* DIBALZO *enveloped in his cloak* (R.)

JAIL. You saved my life, Signor Dibalzo, and I don't forget it; and now I risk mine for you. I should have been drowned in the Bay, if you had'nt pulled me out; and now—(*lowering his voice and coming closer*)—and now I have a good chance of returning the kindness by getting myself hung, or shot. But come this way. (*Stops and listens*)—and be very careful not to raise your voice by any exclamations in Signor Panorio's dungeon, lest a second rope or bullet be provided for yourself. Just mark that.

DIBAL. I shall observe your caution.

JAIL. (*still in a whisper*) You heard the prison-clock strike?

DIBAL. Yes: it struck three. You appointed that hour.

JAIL. It's the safest time. Those who are not then asleep, are not soundly awake—hist!—never mind. When the first quarter strikes, you must flit. Tread softly. These stones have ears. Tongues, too—sometimes.

DIBAL. What's . . .

JAIL. Only the rats.

[*Exeunt* (L. 1st E.)

SCENE III.—[*3rd Entrance.*]

Interior of a Dungeon. The dying and half-naked form of PANORIO *is seen suspended by chains against the wall at some four or five feet from the ground. The dull light of a lamp partially falls upon his head and figure.*

Enter JAILER, *followed by* DIBALZO (R., 1st E.)

DIBAL. (*in a tremulous whisper*) Can this be he? And lives he still?—faugh!—in this charnel air?

JAIL. (*in a whisper*) He was alive an hour ago, and pray'd for a cup of water. I was obliged to give him the queer, sweety-smelling . . . But he often falls into a sort of trance, so that I sometimes fancy his sufferings are all over.

DIBAL. It were far better he died than to live thus. But wherefore this torture?

JAIL. He will not confess who it was that committed the offence for which he is here.

DIBAL. But this he does not know.

JAIL. Ah, that's his misfortune.

DIBAL. See, his breast heaves!

JAIL. (*going*) Hist! you can only have a few minutes.
I'll watch—all ears—outside. [*Exit* JAILER (R.)
  DIBAL. (*advancing gradually*) Alas! my friend—how
    fares it with you?—speak!
        [PANORIO *murmurs a few inarticulate words.*
He moves his drooping head, and his lost mind,
Emerging from the sea of his despair,
Begins again to find life's hideous shore.
Panorio!—speak to me!
  PANO. (*as in delirium*) The languid moon—
Immaculate mother of the angelic stars—
Pours down into the Bay's dark sapphire breast
Funereal silver, o'er the same broad rocks,
Where Helios—cold—cold—shaking back his hair,
Shower'd beams of glory on his favour'd land,
Ere the fierce Samnite smote the Cumæan child—
The verse-embalm'd Parthenope—so cold!
  DIBAL. (*halfaside*) He wanders! and his glassy eyes see
  PANO. O, ice of Caucasus! why do I dream [nought.
Like Epimetheus, while I writhe in bonds
Of the wise Titan?—foresight is in vain,
For where's the use of knowing your own doom?
Sun, moon, earth, ocean ever live the same;
But man, whose ages should increase in light,
Stands still, reels backward, or becomes extinct,
And fossilized may be found.
  DIBAL. (*with anguish*) Panorio!
  PANO. The chill slime of long reptiles as they glide
Over my hands and face, has now become
A kindlier visitation than my thoughts

Of pious Salomba. Let all reptiles live—
So they be harmless.

DIBAL. Pano . . . the damp walls
Have smitten him with deafness.

PANO. (*as if awaking*) Voice!—what voice?
O would I were a many-armed Indian god,
So I could shift these chains to other limbs!
Oh misery! they cut into my bones
By their own weight and mine! (*looking towards* DIBALZO)
What is't stands there?
Substance or shadow—

DIBAL. Oh! (*his voice fails him*)

PANO. Come not, I pray,
To vex a dying man. I well believed
I had already passed. I will not long
Trouble you.

DIBAL. Oh, Panorio! friend! look!
Do you not know me? speak—the moments fly—
I shall be forced away! oh dearest friend,
Do you not know my voice? alas! alas!

PANO. Dibalzo!—yes!—I see you through the film
Of my hot beating eyeballs. Oh, what bliss
To feel these gushing tears!—to hear a voice
Of love and kindness—in my ears how sweet,
Though fast commingling with soft murmurous sounds
Of distant seas on unknown, heavenly shores!

DIBAL. I come—in hopes to aid you—to escape!

PANO. (*with solemnity*) I shall escape: yes, yes, my
    friend, these chains,
Though lock'd, and rivetted into the stone,

Are melting off—or I do melt from them.
Commend me to your lady, and her child—
Her little daughter with the saffron hair—
Why do you weep so?—give my last thoughts to them,
And bless you for this . . . come near—take my hand!
My hand—have you my hand?—no sense of touch
Informs this Spectre—but I see our hands
Are joined, and I am happy. Fare you well,
Dear friend—I have escaped. (*dies.*)

DIBAL. (*after a breathless pause*) He has escaped.
(*kneels in prayer.*)

(*Prison clock strikes the quarter.*)

Re-enter JAILER *softly.*

JAIL. Hist! come away! you must remain no longer!
DIBAL. (*rising solemnly*) Salomba! crown'd assassin!
saintly fiend!
So surely as I live, so sure thou diest!
[*Exeunt* (R.)

END OF THE FIRST ACT.

ACT II.

SCENE I.—[3rd Entrance.]

Apartment in the House of DIBALZO. *Door (upper centre). An ottoman on the left of door.*

Enter ILARIO (R.) *ushering in* GUARINI, *who advances in meditation.*

ILAR. My lady, sir, is well, but very anxious
At the unusual absence—
GUAR. Peace, Ilario:
Signor Dibalzo will be here anon.
Say to my sister I would speak with her.
ILAR. I shall, sir. [*Exit* (U.C.)
GUAR. Inauspicious is the hour,
For this precipitate insurrection.
The subtlest strategy were now in vain
Because too late; inverting so its law
That rashness seems best prudence.
Enter LAURA DIBALZO (U.C.) *with* EDITA *in her arms.*

LAURA. Welcome, my brother.
Rest here awhile, my child. (*placing* EDITA *upon the ottoman*). All night, DIBALZO
Hath been from home—

GUAR. (*in an under tone*) But with important object.
While yesterday the King pass'd thro' the streets
Dibalzo learnt that your dear friend Panorio
Had secretly been seized; so, to his prison
Dibalzo made resolve to penetrate,
By means which he possessed.

LAURA. You make me tremble!

GUAR. 'Tis hazardous no doubt; but well he knows
His presence with his honour now is pledged
For the event at hand. He will take heed.

LAURA. He would return ere this, if he were safe.
How pass those hideous gates? unless to stay
For years within them?—tell me what you think—
(*listening* R.) Dibalzo's voice!

Enter DIBALZO *with clenched hands* (R.)

LAURA. My husband! oh, what moves you thus?

DIBAL. (*speaking through his teeth*). My blood!
And the fierce thoughts of other blood than mine.

LAURA. What do you mean!

DIBAL. That I will kill the King. (LAURA *looks with anxious alarm at* DIBALZO.) Had you last night
Beheld the vision on a dungeon wall,
Which still lives in my brain—and fitfully
Illuminates itself before my eyes,
As vividly as though t'were hanging *there*—
You would not marvel at my words!

LAURA. Alas!
Panorio's dead! is he not?
DIBAL. He is dead.
He sent to you his last remembrances—
And little Edita— [EDITA *awakes, and sits up listening.*
GUAR. (*sadly*) This I apprehended.
DIBAL. (*shaking off his grief*) And at the same time
had you not forseen
Salomba writhing, like a bloody snake
Beneath an armed heel?
LAURA. (*with dismay*) You do not mean—
You will assassinate—
GUAR. (*drily*) Oh no—he means
Only to put an end to the King's murders.
LAURA. (*anxiously to* DIBALZO) You would not kill him?
DIBAL. Most religiously! [*then with steady emphasis.*
'Tis a good deed to kill a wicked King—
Far more to stop a fiend in his career.
LAURA. Not by your hand—not by a blow
Of secrecy?
DIBAL. What matter, so he's slain.
    [LAURA *pauses.* EDITA *lies down again.*
LAURA. You had my heart with you in your design
For insurrection—perilous though it be—
But murder shocks me, and revolts my thoughts!
DIBAL. Look at Edita, there! suppose the despot
Held his knife over her, and you had means
Of instant death—that death you would bestow;
Laura, you know you would. Now, look you here:
Shall we not for our Country—all that breathe

The same air with us—with the same home ties—
The same affections—tenderest kith and kin—
Shall we not for our Country nobly do
As much as for one small domestic tie?

LAURA. The reasoning may be sound, such as it is—
I speak but as I feel—I am but woman.

GUAR. 'Tis palpable to reason; but the world
Cannot appreciate self-devoting acts,
Where private interest hath no lurking place:
Men look into themselves, and don't believe it;
While cradled prejudice with hair on end,
Awakes in terror!

LAURA. Oh, 'tis natural
To shudder at such things. Dibalzo! brother!
Let us not reason on it.

GUAR. (*reflecting*) And besides—
Dibalzo is not all disinterested.

DIBAL. How so?

GUAR. 'Tis vengeance for Panorio's death
That suddenly prompts you.

DIBAL. That's true! and that's right!
Because his death is but the type and proof
Of countless others—why, you cannot doubt it—
Unless we cleave the pinions from this vulture,
And thrust him underground.

LAURA. (*impressively*). Would not the earth
Of that red grave lie heavier on your breast
Than upon his?

DIBAL. No, my dear wife—as light
As perjury on the conscience of a king—

Such kings as ours, I mean, or those who own
A House of Hapsburgh.

GUAR. In this one respect
(I pray you give me leave to shift the subject).
Methinks you wrong their idiosyncracy.
In all affairs between the throne and people,
When bad kings make a solemn vow to God,
They know God understands it.

DIBAL. As a lie!

GUAR. Of State. The people, meaning simple faith,
Are thus at disadvantage. But Dibalzo,
Touching the insurrection you have planned, [*going* (L.)
(No more, my friend of fruitless regicide),
Come to the inner room—let's calmly think
Of what seems now inevitable.

DIBAL. I attend you.
The Marquis Riverola and some friends
Will meet us shortly, and arrange the blow.
Laura, come with me to this conference.
[*Exit* GUARINI (L.)

LAURA. (*hesitating and looking at* EDITA). Edita—

DIBAL. Nay, she sleeps.

LAURA. I scarcely think so.
You know she hath been ill of late. I fear
She is a transient flower.

DIBAL. You are too anxious.
My wife in heart, be thou as true of hand
When for their Country all hands should be raised.
[*Exeunt* (L.)

[EDITA *sits up, and looks after them, while
playing with her long tresses, unconsciously.*

Enter ILARIO (R.)

ILAR. Are you then left alone, my pretty Edita?

EDI. Yes, they are all gone. And I am so frightened.

ILAR. Valentine will be here directly; but why are you frightened, Edita?

EDI. Because papa was telling something out of a Fairy Tale, about a wicked king.

ILA. And what of that?

EDI. And papa said it was a good deed to kill a wicked king. And then papa said he saw a snake under his heel, and mamma was afraid of it.

ILA. (*aside*) A snake under a heel?—kill a king?—what's here? (*in an insinuating tone*) and what else did Signor Dibalzo say?

EDI. Papa said he would do it.

ILA. Do what?

EDI. Kill somebody who was wicked.—Oh, here's Valentine!

Enter VALENTINE (R.) *hastily*.

VAL. (*running to* EDITA) My little Edita—my fairy—my flower! my little star!

EDI. I'm so glad you are come. Will you take me to mamma?

VAL. To be sure I will. You are not well to day?

EDI. Not very well, Valentine.

ILA. (*taking her hand*) Valentine!

VAL. Another time, Ilario (*quickly disengaging herself*).

ILA. You are unkind. If I were not poor, you would smile upon me, perhaps.

VAL. (*playfully*) Then if you love me as much as you

say you do—or (*taking* EDITA *in her arms*) as much as Edita does—why don't you get rich? But it's not the money I should love; only you know, Ilario, we should be a little prudent, as my father says. I am as poor as you are, so we must wait—mus'nt we Edita?

[*Exit, playing with* EDITA *in her arms.*

ILA. Wait 'till I get money? (*thoughtfully*) Methinks I need not wait long if I chose to betray what I have just heard of Signor Dibalzo's designs. For some time I have thought there were secret meetings between himself and several of his friends, and for dark, political purposes; and now the whole truth is pretty clear. There's some plot to kill the King! What a burning secret to fall into the icy hands of a "poor" man—and melt in his craving palms—and that poor man in love—and the girl he loves telling him, while she laughs in his face of beggarly affection, that he is too poor to marry her! So, then, she will take the first man who is rich enough. Can I bear that?—(*after a pause*) What if I made Signor Luca Sforglia aware of this plot? A handsome reward would no doubt be mine, and then Valentine would no longer be able to taunt me with my poverty. (*pauses*) 'Twere a bad business, though. But then, the King is a very devout Sovereign, besides that he reigns by Divine Right and special ordination, and perhaps it was by a miracle that I was vouchsafed the discovery of this intended assassination of so devout a King! (*pauses*). Still, 'tis a bad business. A foul betrayal of a kind master. But then, the temptation—the temptation—and the saving of a devout King through the temptation—

and the feeling that this must be a miraculous intervention? Let me go pray, and confess my sins—and seek holy advice.

    [*Exit* (U.C.) *with a perplexed air.*

SCENE II.—[3rd *Entrance.*]

ORATORY IN THE KING'S PALACE.—*The* KING *seated at a table, writing.* SAN-VOLPE *seated on the right.* SFORGLIA *standing on the left.*

KING. Think you can pounce upon a secret nest
Of sacrilegious conspirators?
 SFOR. I do, my liege.
 KING. (*looking up*) What are the vipers' names?
 SFOR. I do not yet—
 KING. Away! and net them all. [*Exit* SFORGLIA (L).
  (*The* KING *hands a paper to* SAN-VOLPE.)
 SAN-VOL. Your Majesty's Proclamation wisely gives
A due place——
 KING. To Our church, as to Ourself—
"The altar sacrosanct whereon must rest
The destiny of our well-beloved people,
And of Our crown." (*rising*) *A-propos* of Carducci,
Whose head the priest Pelusi packed in salt,
And sent to cheer his co-religionists!
A loyal priest is that—ask him to breakfast.

SCENE III.]   LAURA DIBALZO.   25

SAN-VOL. And for the Proclamation——
KING. We will issue it [friends
Forthwith. And now, to prayers. (*going*) Carducci's
Look'd pleased, methinks, unpacking that *salata*.
[*Exeunt* (R).

SCENE III.—[4*th Entrance.*]

Cloisters of a Deserted Monastery in the Environs of Naples. A Ruined Piazza at the back, over-grown with hanging weeds. Shades of Evening.

Enter SKURDENKA *from the Cloisters.*

SKU. No Synagogue permitted—nor myself
Safe, if my creed be known, would I could grasp
Egypt's seven plagues within my hand, to smite
This Despot King of Naples, who ordains
The worship of some special Deity,
To sanction all his crimes. - O, hypocrite!
Blasphemer of my people and my faith,
The voice that cried in the Old Wilderness
For a straight path, now stings me to the brain,
To strive against this hideous crookedness.
(*looking round*) My friends!
   Enter RIVEROLA *and* BATTHYMAROS (R. 2nd E.)
BATT. Yes, friends
RIVE. (*speaking low*) You are here before the time,
Which shows an earnest spirit in our cause.

SKUR. (*speaking low*) My Country's cause, no less than
BATT. (*in his usual voice*) And mine.   [yours.
Russia and Austria—Satan and his shadow—
Have darken'd all our glories. The bold struggle
Of one succeeding will lead on the rest.
RIVE. (*speaking low*) You are too loud.
BATT. (*good humouredly*) Nay Marquis, I forgot.

Enter DIBALZO *disguised, with two* NOBLES, *from the Cloisters.*

RIVE. (*to* DIBALZO) The word, Sir?
DIBAL. " Laura."
BATT. I had erewhile omitted
The password of your honoured lady's name.
RIVE. Where is Guarini?
DIBAL. He but waits to make
Private arrangements furthering our design.
Letters he hath from Milan, Rome and Venice,
And now sends word to Parma and Bologna.
SKUR. Doth he decide that our first act should be
To slay Salomba?
DIBAL. He admits 'twere right,
But not judicious, looking to results.
SKUR. Right "in the abstract," as some statesmen say,
When they resolve to stand still and look wise.
DIBAL. You do him much injustice in your speech:
Is it not so, my lords?
RIVE. His heart is with us;—
But not his head.   [*The night begins to darken.*
DIBAL. But he will risk that with us.

Enter GUARINI (R. 1st. E.)

RIVE. Signor Guarini?
GUAR. In my sister's name.
DIBAL. Now then at once to settle—
RIVE. But you know,
That several more are coming?
DIBAL. Never mind:
We'll act for them.
GUAR. But first lay down the plan.
BATT. (*laughing quietly*) That's like Dibalzo—he begins with action,
So that all thinking comes too late. [*The night darkens.*
RIVE. Pray, hush!
BATT. (*laughing in a subdued tone*) Who but the ghosts of monks, or bats and owls,
Are like to hear us midst these ruins?
RIVE. Hush!
[*They seat themselves in front of the Cloisters.*
BATT. 'Tis getting dark apace; best light a torch.
[BATTHYMAROS *lights a torch, and sticks it in a fissure of the wall: then seats himself.*
DIBAL. (*rising*) My lords and gentlemen of Italy—
You long have felt and understood the wrongs
Of our loved Country; all the generous efforts
On all sides wasted, and the noble blood
Shed for her on the field, and on the scaffold,
Or by such deaths as vulgar tyranny,
Copying its own degraded mind, intended
For degradation; these high deaths all wasted!

Equally vain the long imprisonments,
Or the excruciating agonies
Of cunning tortures, to extort betrayal
Of patriot friends not yet within their fangs;
And lastly, the foul slanders always coined
To blacken the good name of those who died,
Blighting the sympathy of weak-branch'd hearts,
And swaying back the strong. But if in vain
Our constant efforts, so in vain hath been
The will of all our tyrants. Evermore
We watch, and plot, and rise, e'en while their hands
On fertile scaffolds sow the dragon's teeth.
Blasting and withering is the curse they bring
On us, which surely will revert to them
Heavily multiplied. Now, what's first to do?
You know they constantly proclaim rewards
For the assassination of those men—
Leaders and Chiefs who have escaped their chains.
"Dead, or alive" the royal offer runs—
Minutely specified,—a simple right.
If this is right for them, 'tis right for us;
I therefore do propose that our first act
Should be to slay Salomba.

    RIVE. (*without rising*) I think so too.
    SKUR. And I.   [men?
    DIBAL. (*to the two Nobles*) What say you, noble gentle-
    1st NOBLE. We are of that opinion.
                                    [DIBALZO *seats himself.*
    BATT. So am I—
Provided 'twere not by a light like this!

'Tis not the Magyar's method to do ought
In secrecy, but in the broadest day.
    1st NOBLE. He is too cautious for your honest sword.
    RIVE. (*half aside to* 1st *Noble*) Methinks, an air-gun
        in an opera box—
Standing well back—and with a perfect aim—
Would be——
    1st NOBLE. Or better still . . . (*they talk apart*)
    SKUR. (*pointedly*) Guarini does not speak.
    GUAR. (*rising slowly*) I do not think
Such a beginning good, or politic.
Not good, because the whole world thinks it bad,
In us, who are not royal butchers born.
This is not very wise, but a broad fact,
And therefore would our cause lose sympathy :
Facts last for years—but principles for ages ;
So let us act for some enduring good.
It is not politic, because the deed
Would frighten all our friends of feeble mind,
And cause them to retreat, with all they love,
(Their wealth included) 'neath the poison wing
Of the old despotism, more potent grown
By semblance of paternity. But look
At possible failure in this single blow ?
The patriot's poniard is his own sure death :
Doubtful his blow—still more so, the results
If he strike home. We lose him ; and the act
Will aptly furnish exquisite pretence
For weighty increase of corrosive chains,
With ten-fold difficulties interposed

'Gainst the next rising

DIBAL. (*starting up*) How fail in this blow?
Is not Salomba a mere mortal?

GUAR. No—
Men are deceived in dealing with a king,
Thinking he is a mortal like themselves,
Which is not so, because his influence
By old associations, and the force
Of present interests generant round a throne,
Unnerves the hand, the arm, the planted foot,
And makes the eye's soul-sworn intensity
(Which had been fatal to the best of men)
Miscalculate to the unswerving will.
Meanwhile a thousand other eyes and hands
Watch round the pagod's monomaniac dream.

[DIBALZO *sits down with a dissatisfied air.*

SKUR. The English Shakespeare somewhere paints a
Who felt divinity did hedge him round, [king,
Like to the Glory in the burning bush—
This *ignis-fatuus* of a pestilent swamp. [take

DIBAL. And this were well, for those who choose to
A king at his own value. (BATTHYMAROS *laughs*)

SKUR. (*with a grim laugh*) I would weigh him
Against the worst man that was ever born—
A soul the forfeit of the lesser weight—
And laugh at's lost face, as he kicked the beam!

BATT. (*half in dismay*) Oh!

[*Several others make a simultaneous ejaculation
of a sort of dismay, with a laugh at the
grotesque fury of* SKURDENKA.

GUAR. Let us forbear sardonic levities,
Being sincere men.
   [*A shadowy figure passes through* (R.) *the ruins
   of the piazza at the back. Exit* (L.)
RIVE. (*pointing*) See!—methought I saw—
DIBAL. What?
BATT. Shadows; nothing more.
RIVE. But it moved, I am sure,
And vanished there!
DIBAL. 'Twas but the foliage shaken
By a draughty gust.
SKUR. Or possibly some owl
In search of wisdom.   [*suppressed laughter.*
GUAR. Friends, to the point direct.
I give my vote to spare this tyrant's life,
Save in some open contest. Then 'twere good,
And wise, and worth the pride of upright men,
To trample him, or gibbet high i'the air,—
A new and warning page for history!
Succeeding nobly, Naples will become
The Central altar for all patriot fires. [*sits down.*
BATT. (*rising abruptly*) I am a soldier—clad in the good
Of an illustrious kinsman, basely murder'd— [name
Count Livio Batthymaros, he who bore
A flag of truce from Hungary's Governor,
Into the Emperor's camp, and there was seized,
And, after months of chains, most foully strangled.
What should be thought of me if I held sacred
The life of perjured kings? This same Salomba,
Perjur'd in prayers, with murders on his head—
The thick-set jewels of his bloody crown—

Is placed beyond the scaffold of the law ;
So, let's have justice in the open street !
If aught else is intended, then I plead
The unreasoning prejudices of home life—
Frank habits of a soldier—my own nature,
Which hath a sort of stupid pride in feeling
Its self-approval as the wisest guide—
And therefore with Guarini do I take
My stand against all death-blows in the dark. [*sits down*
    SKURDENKA *rises fiercely.*

SKUR. I am a Pole—and more, a Polish Jew,
Cut to the heart by Austrian perfidies,
And Russia's foulest dealings of all kinds ;
And here in Naples am I doubly cursed—
My creed in heaven and earth impoisoned
With the oppressor's breath. There is no question
If it be good or right to quell this plague !
Stone him to death—cast in a furnace—thrust
Into a den of tigers—we should consider,
Only one thing—not what the ignorant world
Of prating purists (safe themselves) may think,
Write, say or sing of us—but what we men,
I'the thick of all these horrors, really feel
And know—and deem the best to help our cause !
 VOICES. That's right ! right ! right !
   [SFORGLIA, *folded in his cloak, appears at the*
    back of the Cloisters ; the torch-light partially
    falling upon him.
 DIBAL. (*starting up*) Let's talk no more !
    [*All rise and move down in two groups.*

GUAR. (*with energy*) One word!—
It is the cause of our loved Italy—
For whom we all would gladly lay down life,
And peril e'en the soul—one further word!
It is the cause of Hungary and Poland—
Therefore of Europe, and of all mankind;
Let's not endanger it by a doubtful deed—
I pray you—I entreat—

  Voices. Let's talk no more!

  DIBAL. So may all despots perish!

  SKUR. Wholesale assassins! how they laugh in secret
At all such puerile scruples!

        (*General excitement*).

Enter SFORGLIA *slowly from the Cloisters, enveloped in his long cloak—he pauses between the two groups.*

  BATT. Who's this?

  SKUR. Speak!

  DIBAL. (*to* SFORGLIA) Our password sir, so please you?

  SFOR. Death! (*drops his cloak to the ground*).

      (*Guards rush in from Cloisters.*)

  Voices. Betrayed!

(GUARINI *dashes down the torch, which is extinguished.*)

  SFOR. (*to Guards*) Seize them! let none escape!

    [*A rush takes place in the dark* (L.) *and all escape except* DIBALZO, SKURDENKA, *and* BATTHYMAROS.

  DIBAL. (*held between two Guards*) Oh time—so wasted!

SFOR. (*to Guards*) Secure your prisoners! and pursue
    the rest!

[*Exeunt several Guards after* RIVEROLA, GUARINI, &c.

DIBAL. (*sternly*) What next?

SFOR. Oh, you may guess; but for your present solace,
I tell you, sir, your wife—the pass-word "Laura"—
Is safely lodged already.

DIBAL. Laura seized!
But she—she has no knowledge—can say nothing!

SFOR. We shall find means to make the lady speak,
Though she knows nothing. (*to Guards*) To St. Elmo
    straight!

DIBAL. (*with anguish*) A few brief hours invert the
    rational sway
Of great acts, changed to mad acts by delay!

END OF THE SECOND ACT.

ACT III.

SCENE I.—[4th Entrance.]

HALL IN THE KING'S PALACE.—

Enter SFORGLIA (R) *and Officer of the Guard.*

SFOR. (*with a menacing air*) Several escaped, and have
    not yet been found!
OFFI. The darkness, sir——
SFOR. (*sternly*) And have not yet been found!
They *must* be found. Look well to it, all of you,
Or look well to yourselves.   [*Officer bows and exit* (L.)

Enter KING SALOMBA, *attended* (U.C.)

KING. Now Sforglia! (*apart from the rest*) Bring me—
Bring me right soon, a list of all those men,
If not the men themselves. Our sacred life
Is perill'd while of this conspiracy
One winking spark remains—one spark. How is it?
(*suspiciously*) How is it, Sforglia, only three were seized?
    SFOR. My liege, I have increased our spies, and sent
In all directions—I have, moreover, dropt   [them

Hot lead i'the ear of my chief officer,
That for his *own* sake, he should look well to it.
  KING. (*with similar significance*) That's right—
   And you may prudently apply
The like good drops of counsel to *yourself.*
  SFOR. (*rather doubtfully*) My liege——
  KING. Look well to it! [SFORGLIA *bows and exit* (L.)
  KING. (*apart*) I'll do the same myself.
From those I have already in my hands—
And one a woman—I shall find the means
To extort confession of the name and place
Of all who join this plot against Our life,
With revolution following, as of course,
State after State—republics—anarchy.
I'll stop this rolling ball of their small world—
The patriot game—at any rate in Naples.
Dibalzo and his wife, the Pole, the Hungarian,
Shall chronicle in my red book of vengeance,
Not only those who 'scaped, but all their friends,
Down to the last imp of conspiracy.
But first a trial—yes, the form looks well
I'the people's eyes. We'll have an imposing trial;
And I do hope for some new miracle—
Some transubstantial form and fulgency,
Such as my Neapolitan people love—
Commemorative of Our preservation
From the assassins' steel—when they are dead.
    [*Exit* (R.), *Attendants follow.*

SCENE II.—[2nd Entrance.]

A dusky Grove on the Outskirts of Naples. A dark clump of trees at the back.

Enter GUARINI (U.C.)

GUAR. Such is the fate of the self-devoted soul
Who dreams and schemes to raise the incarnate form
Of Italy from the embattled tomb
Wherein her heaving dust is trodden down,
And on whose quick pulsations hath been built
A House of Austria. One day, safe at home,
Happy beside his wife, his children, friends,—
Next day within a loathsome dungeon cast,
Loaded with chains, the martyr vainly broods
On errors of his purpose, judgment, action;
But no repentance undermines his heart,
Or rots the fabric of those noble thoughts
Whose spires pierce through the midnight of his doom.
My sister—brother—and our foreign friends—
What end awaits them ? What else but the scaffold—
Possibly some preliminary tortures—
Salomba's usual course. Can nought be done ?

Enter RIVEROLA.—(R. 1st E.)

RIVE. I'm glad I have found you.
GUAR. Sooth, I know not yet
If 'twere best fly, or hide, or rush on fate
By shouting i'the market, like the patriot—
The valiant half-successful Massaniello.

RIVE. No, no—so promptly you dashed out the torch,
We were not recognized.

GUAR. How know you that?

RIVE. 'Tis sure, or 'ere this I had been arrested,
With many others who are still at large.

GUAR. I'm glad of this, my lord; but as for me,
Suspicion is quite certain. I've no chance
Of safety, but in sudden flight, disguised;—
Yet while my sister and her child are here,
I cannot fly. Whate'er betide, this night
I'll make some effort to set free all those
Who were seized. [purse—

RIVE. How? — name the means? — my life, — my
I will do anything. (*taking* GUARINI's *hand.*)

GUAR. I know it, sir.

RIVE. Speak, then.

GUAR. I have as yet no clear-drawn plan,
But since Dibalzo lately found a way
Into the dungeon of Panorio,
I think 'tis possible by similar means,
To reach Dibalzo, and the rest. (*going* L.)

RIVE. Command me—
And every gentleman who acted with us,—
In all respects. Where shall I meet you next?

GUAR. (*with a melancholy smile*) In heaven, perhaps—
but if still earthly, here!

[*Exeunt* GUARINI (L.), RIVEROLA (R.)

SCENE III.—[4th Entrance.]

HALL IN THE KING'S PALACE *(as before)*. — *Chair of State, with side tables, where* PECCHENDA *and a Secretary are seated writing. Guards at the back. People, and Strangers,—among the latter,* STRONGI'TH'ARM STONEWING.
Trumpets sound.
Enter SALOMBA (U.C.), *attended by* SAN-VOLPE, NÖBLES, SFORGLIA, *Servants, &c.*

KING. (*taking his seat*) Bring in the prisoners!
SFOR. (*hesitating*) Which of them, my liege?
KING. All—one by one—nay, you should understand
I mean the assassins who would raise their hands
(*turning to* SAN-VOLPE) Against the Lord's vicegerent.
SAN-VOL. But of these,
Many lost souls——
KING. (*interrupting*) No doubt—I mean the last.

[SFORGLIA *bows, and exit* (R.U.E.), *followed by Guards.*

KING. (*to* SAN-VOLPE) You are aware that in our [sanctity
Of faith exclusive in the Papal Church,
We have suppress'd the Protestant heresies;
Still more the Greek, and left no tolerance
For the accursed Jew. One of that sect
Leagues with this treasonous horde.
SAN-VOL. He should be burnt.
KING. Well—we shall see what's best.

Re-enter SFORGLIA *and two Guards, with* DIBALZO *in chains: he is placed in front* (R). *Enter* BATTHYMAROS *in chains with two guards. He is placed on the left of* DIBALZO. *Enter* SKURDENKA *in chains with two guards. He is placed in front* (L).

PECC. (*slowly rising with papers*) My liege——
KING. Not yet. (PECCHENDA *bows, and re-seats himself*)
That our paternal life and constant prayers,
Our known devotion and attendance close
On all the offices o' the Church—her rites,
Her forms, her penances, and miracles,
May add thereto the bless'd desire to show
Mercy unto all shades of innocence,
We ask you, are you innocent? If so,
In what degree? (*turning to* DIBALZO.)

DIBAL. The highest—having thought
To do no wrong. [perhaps?

KING (*with malicious smoothness*). To do some good,
(*To* SFORGLIA) Bring in the witness.

[*Exit* SFORGLIA (R. U. E.)

(*to* BATTHYMAROS) You would say the same?

BATT. (*bluntly*) Your Majesty, I prefer to say nothing.

KING (*to* SKURDENKA). And you? (SKURDENKA *haughtily turns his head aside. The King leans towards* SAN-VOLPE.) I'll bend this Polish Israelite.

Re-enter SFORGLIA. (R.U.E.) *He stands aside. Enter* LAURA, *followed by two guards. She advances to the centre.*

DIBAL. (*aside*) My wife, the witness!

KING (*to* LAURA, *while pointing to* BATTHYMAROS). Do you know that man? (BATTHYMAROS *advances two paces.*)

LAURA. My liege, I do not. (BATTHYMAROS *steps back*)

KING (*pointing to* SKURDENKA). Dost know that other?

LAURA. I do not, sire; though I have seen him once.

KING. Where?

LAURA. At a distance.

KING (*pointing to* DIBALZO). Do you know that man?

LAURA. Happily I did—Your Majesty. (*she weeps.*)

KING. And now
With sorrow?

LAURA. And a wife's devotedness,
Surpassing any sorrow.

KING. Is it so? [Majesty

LAURA (*drying her eyes*). What other answer did your
Expect from me?

KING. (*to* PECCHENDA) Proceed.

PECC. (*rising, and reading from a paper*) Claudio Dibalzo—Meszlenki Batthymaros—and Michael Skurdenka,—you are severally and collectively accused of the heinous and most wicked crime of high treason;— to wit, that you did all three plot, conspire, and devise means to compass the death of our most sanctified and lawful sovereign, Ognissanti Salomba, King of Naples; and furthermore, that you had intended to incite, or to endeavour to incite the Populace of this city, and of the Country round about, to rebellion and insurrection; and furthermore, that you had it in view, if the primary high treason and wickedness had succeeded, to incite other States of Italy to revolt and rebel against their liege Sovereigns, Conquerors, and Rulers, and to assist those rebels in the same with arms, or armed men, and with shelter and protection if needed. Now, of these crimes, or one or more of these crimes, you Claudio Dibalzo, you Meszlenki Batthymaros, and you Michael Skurdenka, stand accused. Do you confess your gilt or deny it, or do you plead by any extenuating circumstances that you are only guilty in certain degrees?

DIBAL. By whom are we accused?

PECC. By the woman there!

LAURA. By *me*!

DIBAL. Do the forms of your office prevent you from knowing that that woman is a lady, and therefore incapable of such baseness?

PECC. Lady—wife—and woman—Laura Dibalzo is the accuser in this case.

LAURA (*firmly*). Laura Dibalzo *is* an accuser in this case;—and she accuses *you*, and those who prompted you to this atrocity, of uttering a gross and most unfounded falsehood.

PECC. The statement is *well* founded.

LAURA (*with calm firmness*). Will your Majesty allow such a tongue to continue?

PECC. Did you never utter words to the effect—or which might be *construed* to the effect—that your husband proposed to kill the king?

LAURA (*contemptuously*). I utter words to be construed to the effect?

PECC. You were overheard to say as much in your cell last night.

LAURA. To whom? I was alone.

PECC. To yourself.

LAURA (*smiling with derision*). When I was asleep?

PECC. Perhaps—but dreaming.

LAURA. Wretches that ye are! Is tyranny come to such a pass that the loving wife of a noble husband is not safe from spies, even when she dreams of him in the patriots' dungeon!

PECC. You admit this dream, then?

LAURA (*with perplexed anguish*). Wretches!

PECC. Remember the respect and awe due to the presence of His Majesty, who vouchsafes this special trial. You are not in an ordinary Court of Law.

LAURA (*weeping*). Indeed I perceive that, very plainly. I am vexed at these tears—they are not grief.

PECC. Shame, rather.

LAURA (*with dignity*). No; pride in myself as a true wife—awake or asleep. (*to the King, with pathos*) We are all in the hands of God—Your Majesty. May we never tremble at feeling this.

KING (*disturbed*). Be silent, woman. (*To* SFORGLIA) Call a better witness. Heaven assist us!

[*Exit* SFORGLIA *with two Guards*, (R. U. E.)

KING (*to* BATTHYMAROS). You are from Hungary?

BATT. (*stepping forward*) Your Majesty, I am.

KING. An exile?

BATT. Certainly.

KING. Therefore a traitor.

BATT. (*with soldier-like ease*) Oh, no, Sire—a patriot. The only traitors in Hungary were of the House of Hapsburgh. As for the Croatian traitor, Jellachich, (before he became the favourite blood-hound of the Emperor of Austria) or such men as Gorgey and Haynau —Haynau who caused women to be flogged, and was afterwards flogged himself by honest brewer's men in London . . . . .

KING. Peace, Magyar rebel!

BATT. But . . . . [*guards thrust him back into his place. He folds his arms with a smile.*

Re-enter SFORGLIA (R.U.E.) *He stands aside. Enter* ILARIO *guarded. He remains at the back.*

LAURA. (*aside*) Ilario!

DIBAL. (*aside*) Villain!—but what can he know?

PECC. (*To Ilario*) Were you valet to Signor Dibalzo?

ILAR. I was.

PECC. Do you see him among the prisoners here?
(*Ilario drops his head*). Do you see him?

ILAR. Yes—there! (*pointing without raising his head*).

PECC. Did you not hear him propose to kill His Majesty, our most devout and sacred Sovereign?

ILAR. No—never.

KING. (*with affected astonishment*) How's this!

ILAR. I never did.

KING. (*to Pecchenda—then turning to San-Volpe*) We have been mistaken, it would seem?

PECC. Did you not, at least, glean an indirect whisper of his treasonous designs?

LAURA. Will your Majesty permit me to ask what value can be attached to the least gleaning of an indirect whisper?

KING. (*impatiently*) Dismiss this indirect, inadequate witness! Your evidence breaks down. (*To Sforglia*) You must release the prisoners!

(*Sensation of gladness in the Court.*)

PECC. My liege—*one* other witness.

KING. Let it be the last. (*hypocritically*) They appear to be innocent.

(STRONGI'TH'ARM *and others applaud.*)

[*Exeunt* ILARIO, SFORGLIA, *and Guards*, R. U. E.

KING (*to* SKURDENKA). You are from Warsaw, as we learn?

SKUR. I am from Warsaw.

KING. Your uncle was a rich Jew in Praga, and your father a Rabbi; but they both lost all their possessions by the insurrection, excited by one of the mad French revolutions.

SKUR. They lost nought, O King—they freely *gave* their wealth to aid the struggle of their country against Russia. All the citizens, joyfully, and as one man, did the same.

KING. (*to* SAN-VOLPE) We had not thought the Poles such fools.

SKUR. (*to* SAN-VOLPE) The wisdom of this world is far more foolish. (*to the* KING) Your Majesty may remember that some of your own countrymen had the same public feeling. The brave and single minded people of Leghorn offered the whole of their possessions to preserve the liberty of a single state of Tuscany.

KING. Peace, infidel!

[SKURDENKA *turns aside scornfully*).

Re-enter SFORGLIA. (R. U. E.) *He stands aside. Enter a Guard bearing* EDITA *in his arms. He stands back.* LAURA *and* EDITA *open their arms to each other.* DIBALZO *stands confounded and perplexed*).

LAURA. (*advances*) My child! (SFORGLIA *prevents her approach*) What would you do?

SFOR. No harm—no injury.

LAURA. Then let me take her!

PECC. No—no. She has to say something.

LAURA. Say what? She can speak better in my arms. I will be silent. I will not prompt her by a word or pressure—let me—

PECC. It must not be.

LAURA (*aside*). Oh my bursting heart! What would they—

KING. Let the child speak! Assure her of all safety.

SAN-VOL. (*to* LAURA) The King's august protection.

LAURA (*aside*). What can she say?

PECC. (*to* EDITA *in a mild tone*) Are you the daughter of that lady?

EDITA. Yes—yes—let me go to her.

SFOR. (*softly*) Not yet—but presently.

EDITA. There is my father—let me come to you!

DIBAL. (*aside, doubtfully*) What can she possibly—?

KING (*mercifully*). Take the child to her mother's arms.

(*Sensation and applause in the Court*).

(LAURA *steps forward a few paces, and the Guard places* EDITA *in her arms. They embrace.* LAURA *and* DIBALZO *watch* EDITA *with intense anxiety and painful perplexity.*)

PECC. Speak freely, child Edita. Did you ever hear your father tell you a Fairy Tale about a man who wanted to kill somebody?

LAURA. A fairy tale!—Oh monstrous!

KING. Silence! You promised silence.

EDITA (*to* PECCHENDA). Oh yes, I did once.

PECC. When?

EDITA. A little time ago. I was laid to sleep on the ottoman; but I was not asleep.

PECC. You were not asleep.—Well?

EDITA. No; I only kept quiet because I thought mamma wished me to do so.

DIBAL. (*aside*) What's this!—what's coming?

PECC. She wished you. Did she say so?

EDITA. Oh no; I only thought she wished.

PECC. And what did your father say?

LAURA (*agitated beyond bearing*). He said—he said—you were his dear little Edita

SFOR. (*in an under tone of menace*) Be silent, for your child's sake.

EDITA (*her eyes filling with tears as she turns to* LAURA). O yes—he often said that—and you too, mamma! I was always your dear little Edita.

PECC. (*very softly*) What was the Fairy Tale about?

STRONGI'TH'ARM. (*aside*) Cruel—very cruel.

EDITA. I do not know what it was—do you, mamma?

PECC. But who was meant?

EDITA. Indeed I cannot tell.

PECC. Why not?

EDITA. Because I do not know.

PECC. But what did your father say?—what words did he use?

EDITA (*twining her fingers fondly in her mother's hair, and looking in her face*). Oh, papa said it would be a good deed to kill a wicked king.

> [*General sensation.* LAURA *covers her face convulsively with both hands. In dismay and anguish she lets* EDITA *slip from her arms.* DIBALZO *hastily catches her up, and embraces her with despairing tenderness.* LAURA *is borne off fainting* (L.)
>
> (*The King rises. All rise.*)

KING. We are the King he meant; and mere waste wind,
For such as he, have been our prayers;—waste also
Fastings, endowments, penances, chapels built,
All miracles foster'd, life immaculate—
Or almost so;—these rebels' eyes invert
Both God's high throne, and man's. Lead them away,
Each to his dungeon!—load them with rough chains,
Till they are brought forth to be stretch'd beneath
The traitors' heaven-sent stone!

> [*Exeunt* SALOMBA, SAN-VOLPE, NOBLES, PEC-CHENDA,*Secretary,People,Strangers,&c.*(U.E.)
>
> [*Officer and Guards lead away* DIBALZO, BAT-THYMAROS, *and* SKURDENKA (L. 2nd E.)

(*Edita utters a cry, and wrings her hands, being now in the arms of a guard, with Sforglia standing by.*)

Re-enter LAURA *wildly* (L.)

LAURA. What dreadful dream! (*Edita hides her head*)
What stupor sings and curdles in my brain!
Death! crush'd beneath—my husband crush'd to death!
And by my child's unconscious parricide!
O, miserable child! O, fatal voice,
So sweet in murdering him who gave thee life,
And her who gave thee birth and nutriment,
And ever tender love!—Oh! dull of sense
And filial instinct, so to keep awake
When thou shoulds't sleep—or, being awake, to hold
The memory of words thou should'st have lost!
Thou shoulds't have said—thou—Oh no, no, my girl
Edita—[*clasping* EDITA *in her arms*] you spake well and
  right. Your father
Did say t'was good to kill a wicked king—
And you repeated nothing but—the *truth*! [remark.

SFOR. (*significantly*) She also may repeat that last

LAURA (*deliriously*). No need, sir—*you* can do it, and
             ['tis likely
The same will ring in echoes thro' the night,
While grovelling ears are at my dungeon door—
Thou busy abortion of a childless Throne!

            [*Exeunt* (R.)

END OF THE THIRD ACT.

E

ACT IV.

SCENE I.—[2nd Entrance.]

Grove on the outskirts of Naples (as in SCENE 2, ACT III.) *Distant music of a mass, but vocal only. Sound of bells. Peasants in holiday dresses pass across to attend the festival of San Stefano.*

Enter GUARINI, *disguised, and* VALENTINE, *from the clump of trees.*

GUAR. Do you believe, my good girl, that the remorse of Ilario is as deep as he professes?

VAL. Indeed Signor, I am sure of it.

GUAR. May not his present proposal to assist me in the liberation of Signor Dibalzo, my sister, and our foreign friends, be the consummation of his treachery?

VAL. Oh no, Signor: Ilario is most truly penitent.

GUAR. What he did was through his love for you, in hopes of a reward which should enable him to marry you?

VAL. It was, Signor: I also am to blame, having taunted him with his poverty.

GUAR. And now he has gold?

VAL. No, no, no—Ilario is as poor as ever. The Government refused the proclaimed reward, and made him a jailer instead. But I have promised to forgive him, if he will truly assist you, in conjunction with the other jailer you have spoken with, in the liberation of my lady and the Signor Dibalzo.

GUAR. And our Polish and Hungarian friends?

VAL. Doubtless, if possible. Besides this, my father, Cyrille, will accompany you. He is an exile in the cause of liberty, and can feel for those who suffer here. He is a locksmith, you know, and may be useful.

GUAR. And he will risk this attempt?

VAL. He will—he will. He shall speak to you himself. He waits yonder. [*makes signs off* (L.) *and Exit* (L.)

GUAR. (*thoughtfully*) The patriotic son of a brave and inconsistent people. Modern Rome can never forgive Paris, or at least her soldiers.

Enter CYRILLE (L.)

CYR. (*roughly, but respectfully*) My daughter, Sir, has trusted her old father: so may you.

GUAR. (*looking steadfastly at him*) I do—for myself—and I think I may for others. Your name is Cyrille?

CYR. Cyrille Le Brun. I am a locksmith. I have a strong hand, and I know my craft.

GUAR. You wasted good blood at some of the barricades, I think?

CYR. I lost some. I did not *waste* it.

GUAR. Enough, my friend. You'll go with me to the prison as soon as night sets in.

E 2

CYR. I will. Which prison?—there are many here.

GUAR. Saint Elmo. Every monstrous thing here is under the special protection of a Saint. (*pausing*) You are aware that you risk your head with mine in this business?—and, to be frank with you, you have but little prospect of reward, because, if it succeed, we must instantly fly. [*Evening begins to darken.*

CYR. I am aware it may cost my life; but as my daughter's lover betrayed you, to get money for *her*, I wish to add my mite——

GUAR. (*taking his hand*) Your life—brave honest heart!

CYR. (*with emotion*) My mite, to increase his penitence. So, no more. (*going*) Now to our disguises. I will provide them. Something military or monastic. Of all dark disguises, a monk's hood lies in the smallest compass.

GUAR. While it compasses the largest space in Naples.

(*Night comes on*) [*Exeunt* (L.)

SCENE II.—[4th Entrance.]

A dismal passage in the prison of St. Elmo. A small grated portal at the back (R.)

Enter LAURA *mournfully* (R. 2nd E.)

LAURA. My husband is not dead—not yet—I know
I shall feel something sudden in the air,
When his last breath exhales. Will my heart hold—
Or break at once? or will my brain turn sick,
And hurried words of self-discourse within,
Sink eddying to a void? All's one to me.

Why should Salomba spare my life, and promise
My liberty in a few days?—alas!
When I go forth, the world to me is blank.
I seek my house—no husband will be there—
No brother's voice—what is that house to me,
But vacancy and anguish? There the seat,
Wherein Dibalzo sat—the window, there,
Where oft he stood in converse with my brother,
Whose penetrating, earnest voice so oft
Spake of our Italy, while framing plans
Of noblest scope. And when at night I seek
My widow's bed, Dibalzo's shade will clasp
This phantom of despair—so late a wife!
(*after a pause*) When I go forth alone—ah! yes, alone!
Edita! where art thou, my child? the wretches
Still keep her from me—she will die—will die!

Enter SAN-VOLPE (R. U. E.) *with a solemn and devout air.*

SAN-VOL. *Angelis suis Deus mandavit de te!*
LAURA. I attend you, reverend father. [ear—
SAN-VOL. O, Daughter, it hath reach'd my gladden'd
Thrice gladden'd at the pious innocence,
Which, though by guilt beset, sustain'd thy soul—
That in the secret conference at thy house,
Touching the murder of our sacred King,
Thy voice opposed the sacrilegious deed. [heard—
LAURA. I know not what your reverence may have
My brother—each of us—
SAN-VOL. I understand.
You seek to screen your husband: but in vain.
Tis well proved what *he* said.

Laura. Can nothing save him?

San-Vol. Nothing that I can do—or that I should—
But *you* may save him.

Laura. I!—oh tell me how?

San-Vol. There must be executions—scaffold scenes—
Death, all aghast and shuddering at himself,
Writing red warnings with his proper hand:
Wherefore the Hungarian, and the infidel Jew,
Must die, and strike a terror in their ends.
'Tis a high privilege, passing their deserts,
Thus to assist the future preservation
Of our most holy King.

Laura. His Majesty
Would surely show more holiness by mercy?

San-Vol. Not so. Salomba by divine law reigns:
Ordain'd by Heaven—Vicegerent of our God—
A special providence bids him do Heaven's will,
Of which he is the best interpreter,
Through his communion with the Church.

Laura. Ah me!
My brain and pulse beat not in harmony.
But how to save my husband?

San-Vol. By obedience
To thine own conscience. Since thou saw'st t'was sin
To plot against Salomba's spotless life,
Thou wilt an equal virtue comprehend
In some ecstatical and conspicuous act
Of public thanksgiving that the wicked shafts
Were intercepted, and the traitors foil'd.
Wilt thou do this? (*with tender exhortation*)

LAURA. (*anxiously*) Dibalzo being saved?

SAN-VOL. Spared, thou would'st say.

LAURA. His life—will that be spared?

SAN-VOL. This has been promised. Canst thou hesitate?
What are those men to thee—Magyar or Pole?
No dear friends bringing radiance to thy house,
But men thou never knew'st until they stood
In open court as regicides accurs'd.

LAURA (*with painful perplexity*). What form of prayer?

SAN-VOL. This shall be given thee
To study, and repeat with uprais'd arms,
Attired in white, set high above the crowd.

LAURA. In white?

SAN-VOL. Art thou not penitent?

LAURA. Set high?
What, holy father, may this mean?

SAN-VOL. (*indifferently*) It means
A pedestal beneath some holy roof—
Perchance among stone statues—possibly
On vapour-veil'd plinth,—or in a cupola
Uplifted near the arch, midst fumes of smoke!

LAURA. (*agitated*) But this might be mistaken—and
Miraculous? [appear

SAN-VOL. (*looking down*) Do you think so?

LAURA. Altar-smoke?

SAN-VOL. Not from the altar, for a regicide.

LAURA. (*indignantly*) No!—no! I understand it now!
[*She retires several paces.*

SAN-VOL. (*sternly*) Beware!

LAURA. Thick, yellow, whirling, suffocating smoke,
Out of which issues screams of those who burn,
To mingle with my penitential prayers!
While I am white-robed for a hellish lie!
Merciful God! I cannot do this thing!
   SAN-VOL. Heretic!—the stake may vibrate soon with
      thee!   [*Exit* (R.)
   LAURA (*recovering herself*). If I had done this—e'en
      to save his life,
My husband's voice had thunder'd thro' the prayer,
And I had died—all hopeless—on the spot—
Swinging from wires amidst the frantic smoke,
Aiding this mockery of Heaven and Nature!
If we must die, be it like men and women,
And not like mummers in a blasphemous show!
      (*relapsing into languor*)
I have been stunn'd, methinks—drunk the mad wine
Of too great misery, else I had not found
The strength to bear so much. There's more to come.
Well, let it come. Last night I dreamt, a face
Bloom'd from the earthy darkness, like a flower
Seeking heaven's birthday light, and with a look,
Like that of lovers, trembling on the verge
Of the first kiss. Methinks some angel thus, [ready!
Was sent half way to greet me. (*waving her hand*) I am
   (*Sinks on a seat. Then listening, and looking
      towards the grated portal* R.)
The sound of footsteps!
   (*The* JAILER *and two other figures appear behind
      the grating.*)
Strangers with the Jailer!

Enter JAILER *cautiously, through the portal, followed by* GUARINI *in a military cloak, and* CYRILLE *in a monk's hood.*

GUAR. (*in an undertone*) Sister, brief greeting!

LAURA (*throwing herself into* GUARINI'S *arms*). My brother! why have you ventured——

GUAR. (*hurriedly to* JAILER) Which is Dibalzo's dungeon?

JAIL. Yonder is the door; but it is not in my charge.

GUAR. In the charge of Ilario?

JAIL. (*hurriedly*) No—another man, whom Ilario has drawn away; but we could not obtain the key from him.

GUAR. No matter: a friend here will find one.

CYR. (*in a gruff voice*) Key!—no need. I'll take off the lock—or the hinges. (*pointing off* L.) That door?

[*Exit* (L. 3rd E.)

LAURA (*excitedly*). You will effect Dibalzo's escape?

GUAR. And yours.

LAURA. Now?

GUAR. This moment. (*to* JAILER) Where are the dungeons of the Polish and Hungarian prisoners?

JAIL. (*doggedly*) Not in my charge. (*aside*) I dare not venture so far as that.

GUAR. But where are they?

JAIL. I do not know.

GUAR. What detains Cyrille? (*looking off* (L.)

JAIL. The lock cannot be opened, and your man will have to unscrew, or wrench, or cut through. He will need your assistance.

GUAR. (*hastening off*) Oh, for a giant's hand!
[*Exit* (L. 3rd. E.)

JAIL. (*approaching* LAURA) The Signor Guarini designs to carry you safe out of this prison with your husband?

LAURA. He this instant said so.

JAIL. Aye: I agreed to assist him, in conjunction with the new jailer, Ilario, now watching outside—as far as Signor *Dibalzo* is concerned; but you cannot *both* escape —for several reasons.

LAURA. Oh, wherefore not?

JAIL. (*hurriedly*) There are too many in your party already. Only one at a time can go—you and your husband must therefore agree upon this.

LAURA. Agree!—oh, I decide at once. Let *him* escape! (*with emotion*) Besides, I could not leave my child.

JAIL. You consent to remain, then?

LAURA. I will insist upon it. (*clasping her hands firmly*)

JAIL. No—that will cause delay. Hide behind that buttress. I will say you are gone already by that door.
[*pointing to the portal.*

LAURA (*affectionately*). Do your best for him.
[LAURA *retires behind a buttress, and the* JAILER *swings open the grated portal.*

Re-enter GUARINI *with* DIBALZO *hastily, followed by* CYRILLE, *with one hand bound up. All speak in an undertone and rapidly.*

DIBAL. Where is my wife? (*looking round*)

JAIL. (*pointing to the open portal*) Gone on before you—as I directed her.

DIBAL. (*hurrying towards the portal — and stopping short*) But where are our friends—the Hungarian and the Pole?

JAIL. I cannot help them.

DIBAL. (*to* GUARINI) Then we should remain, and let them fly!

GUAR. That's true. (*To* JAILER) Quick! where are they?

JAIL. I do not know. (*aside*) And I will not know.

GUAR. You do not?

JAIL. Moreover, I have to think of my own neck. At any rate I cannot do more *to-night*.

DIBAL. To-morrow night?

JAIL. Yes—yes—to-morrow—but now the minutes fly, and so must you! like the lady who has fled before you!

DIBAL. We must overtake her!

> [CYRILLE *passes through the portal, then* DIBALZO, *and the* JAILER *is urging* GUARINI *to follow* DIBALZO, *when a clash of arms is heard* (L.)

JAIL. Back! back! (*all hurry back*) The night-guard has taken some alarm! (*listening and looking towards* L.) We cannot now go by the portal passage!—We must fly another way. (*pointing* L. 1st E.) There! (*Exeunt* DIBALZO *and* GUARINI) Leave the portal staring widely open to deceive them. (CYRILLE *does this*) Follow!

> [*Exeunt* JAILER *and* CYRILLE (L. 1st E.)

(*clash of advancing Guards*)

Enter SFORGLIA *with* OFFICER *and Guards* (L. 3rd E.)

SFOR. Villains!—the locks and fastenings cut away!—treachery!—where is the Jailer!—and the new Jailer, Ilario!—but first pursue!

OFFR. (*looking round*) In what direction?

Re-enter LAURA *from behind the buttress. She hastily closes the portal, to deceive them, passes the long bolts, and places herself in front.*

SFOR. Ha!—onward through the portal!

(OFFICER *and Guards advance*)

LAURA (*with passion*). Stand back!

SFOR. Drag her away!

LAURA. Victims! stand back! lost victims, I tell you a mine is beneath your feet, and in an instant, when I apply this match, you will be all blown into the air!

(*Guards hesitate in alarm.*)

SFOR. She has no match! there's no mine here! tear her away! [OFFICER *and Guards seize* LAURA.

LAURA. Keep back, ye accurst of Heaven, and all the Saints! do you not hear the rumbling of the earthquake under your *very feet?* Vesuvius will speak louder to you anon! (*clinging to the grating*)

SFOR. She raves! cut off her arms, if she will not let go!

(OFFICER *raises his sword.*)

LAURA. (*like a martyr*) Cut them off! Heaven gives me fortitude to bear it!

SFOR. Be it so!—fools, do you hesitate!—hack her to pieces! (*draws his sword*)

LAUR. (*Guards advancing*) But the King! remember the King!—he has not ordered my death yet! he reserves me for some *torture!* (*they hesitate*) You did not think of that!

SFOR. (*furiously*) Her raving will enable the traitors to escape!—away with her! away with her!

[LAURA *is dragged away* (R.) *by* OFFICER *and two Guards.* SFORGLIA *and Guards then rush into the portal, and Exeunt* (*i.e. in the wrong direction*). LAURA, *fainting, but with a satisfied air, is borne off* (R.) *by* OFFICER *and two Guards.* [*Exeunt* (R.)

SCENE III—[2nd *Entrance.*]

A Vineyard at the foot of Vesuvius; part only of the Mountain-slope is seen—Sunrise.

Enter two OLD VINTAGERS (L.)

1st V. I prayed every night all the winter long for a good grape season, and see, we have got it!

2nd V. But not through *your* prayers, old Isaco; for I, and my wife and five daughters, prayed constantly—morning, noon and night did we—ha! (*looking off* L.) didn't we?   [*music of pipe and tambourine outside.*

Enter VINTAGE WOMEN, GIRLS *and* BOYS (L.)

2nd V. Didn't we all pray hard for a good vintage?

Voices. All prayed constantly—to San Gennaro.

1st G. And often in the Saint's own Chapel!

2nd G. And to many other Saints!

3rd G. And they heard every word we said to ourselves as we knelt!

2nd G. Look at these gold chains and things!—all given me for my prayers!

Voices. And look at mine!—look at these!

[*Exeunt* (R.) WOMEN, GIRLS, *and* BOYS, *with music of pipe and tambourine.*

2nd V. (*after a moody pause*) Your prayers help the harvest?

1st V. (*fiercely*) Yes, I said so!

2nd V. Phoo! *mine* were the sort of prayers to bring down the sunlight, and they did it!

1st V. You're a liar!

2nd V. (*half drawing his knife*) Say that again!

1st V. You're a liar!

Enter STRONGI'TH'ARM STONEWING (L.) *with a note-book in his hand.*

2nd V. I'll wait for you. [*Exit* (R.)

STRONGI'TH'ARM. A hot quarrel in this lovely vineyard?

1st V. Why not here as well as anywhere else, Signor?

STRONGI'TH'ARM. And about what, may I ask?

1st V. He said his prayers were heard a hundred times better than mine!

STRONGI'TH'ARM. How could he possibly know that? Do not quarrel with such a mountain of ignorance.

1st. V. No, I quarrel with his eruptions.

STRONGI'TH'ARM. He will be sorry for his eruptions the next time he is upon his knees. Now, if besides praying for the ripening of your grapes, you would sometimes pray for the twenty thousand of your countrymen groaning and shivering in yonder dungeons for political offences—many of them being quite innocent—some who have never been even examined—and some who are well *known* to be innocent—surely heaven would be more pleased with such practical Christianity?—now don't you think so?

1st. V. (*doggedly*) Oh, I don't know. Our King is a holy man. Christianity! (*going*) Said he'd wait for me.

[*Exit* (R.) *drawing his knife.*

STRONGI'TH'ARM. While the gross superstitions and " the horrors with which the government is, at this time, carried on, are like the negation of God erected into a system of political rule," it is no wonder that the people become brutalized and fanatical by the highest examples. (*starting*) I hope the King will not—fancy—and take it into his head to have me arrested on suspicion? Perhaps I had better burn my note-book? But with all those wretched prisoners!—No: I will risk it.

[*Exit* (L.) *secreting his note-book.*

SCENE IV.—[3rd Entrance].

Gloomy passage in the prison of Saint Elmo. Three dungeon doors, with long bolts, and a small grating in each. A dull lamp hangs from the wall.

Enter SFORGLIA *and* SAN-VOLPE (R.), *followed by four Guards, who stand back.*

SAN-VOL. I found Dibalzo's wife—the traitress Laura,
So contumacious and so lost to grace
That e'en the promise of her husband's life
Could not obtain consent to do the penance
Vouchsafed her. Wherefore our lord the King directs
You work upon her through her *child*, to find
The knowledge he requires.
 SFOR. Most reverend father,
It shall be done.
 SAN-VOL. Touching the other two—(*pointing to two of the dungeon doors*).
Magyar and Pole—one might administer
Such unapparent influence as should lower
Proud temperaments . . . . . um?
 SFOR. *Atropos bella donna,*
Last night i'the water-cruse . . . .
 SAN-VOL. (*raising one hand*) Oh fie!—The King
Reserves the woman as a last resource.

SFOR. So I anticipated, holy Father. [last words,
SAN-VOL. The others, try once more. Should their
Despite thy drugs, their hunger, cold, and chains,
Grow fierce, give them free scope. Passion doth utter
More secrets than pure reason; as the rays,
Concentred and intense, betray the scales
Of dragons lurking midst hot fens and rocks,
Far clearer than the broad and general beams
Which ripen harvests. Let them vent their fury.
SFOR. I shall observe your counsel, reverend father;
And failing, or succeeding, bring to an end.
SAN-VOL. (*extending his hands over Sforglia's head*)
Panem angelorum manducabit homo!
[*Exit* (R.)
SFOR. (*to Guards*) Lead forth the prisoner, Meszlenki Batthymaros.
[*Exeunt two Guards into dungeon* (R.)
SFOR. With doleful tones he sung, and towards mid-
Fought his last fight in feeble fantasy. [night,
The drug hath done its work.

Enter BATTHYMAROS *from dungeon, partly supported by a Guard.*

SFOR. Now, prisoner—mark!
A last hope yet remains!
BATT. (*faintly*) For Hungary?
SFOR. No—for yourself. Name your accomplices! Speak!

F

BATT. (*trying to rouse himself*) Speak?—Of what?
SFOR. Name your accomplices! [my speech.
BATT. (*languidly*) Better, my friend, that I should lose
SFOR. Your head!—you will lose that.
BATT. (*with a sick careless air*) Well then—'tis lost!
SFOR. Where is Dibalzo?
BATT. Somewhere safe—I hope.
SFOR. (*in a friendly tone, and placing one hand on Batthymaros' shoulder*) I hope so, too; but there's no need to fly,
Or to secrete himself, unless beneath
The fountain of mercy.
BATT. (*forcing a laugh*) Meaning your King, or Pope!
But I suspect they've found a safer fountain.
SFOR. (*aside*) A safer fountain? (*aloud*) Come now, at once—the men
Who would have kill'd the King?
BATT. (*rousing himself*) I!
SFOR. All their names!
BATT. My own name. [friend!—
SFOR. (*in a whisper*) Hush!—be wise!—I am your (*taking his hand*) I was myself once a republican.
BATT. (*withdrawing his hand languidly*) Do not insult me—I feel sick at heart—
And my knees fail—take me back to my dungeon.
SFOR. (*loudly*) Name your accomplices, or your end is come!
BATT. (*languidly*) To my dungeon. (*turning to go*)
SFOR. To your grave, if you refuse.
BATT. Do not insult me.

SFOR. Take back the oaf, awhile!

> [*Batthymaros, with submissive languor, is led back to his dungeon.*

Bring forth the woman!

> [*Exeunt two Guards through the door of the second, or central, dungeon.*

SFOR. (*thoughtfully*) A safer fountain?—he expects they have found?

Re-enter Guards, with LAURA *from dungeon.*

LAURA (*after a pause*). Why am I thus led out?—
unless to die?
Give me some tidings of my child, I pray you!
The holy father, who was angry with me,
Hath surely not deserted us. He promised
Dibalzo's life!

SFOR. Conditionally. You refused. (*advancing savagely*)
'Tis well to mention this, after assisting
His late escape!

LAURA. In that I only did
What every wife should do.

SFOR. Not for a traitor:
But I have other matter for you now.
Dibalzo being gone—and safe—no doubt—
You can have little care for those who join'd him,
And first, perhaps, suggested the vile plot
Which nearly cost his head. Who were these men?
Nobles or merchants—scholars or lazzaroni? . . . .
You do not answer. Will you not reply?

LAURA (*with a fixed look*). What would *you* do—if you
    stood in my place?

SFOR. 'Tis not an answer.

LAURA. No, sir, 'tis a question.

SFOR. Well—I would not condemn my *child* to death.

LAURA (*with sudden terror*). Oh!— You—you do not

SFOR. Certainly.   [mean it!

LAURA. (*wildly*) My child! injure my child!—one
    wholly innocent!

The child whose very innocence had caused
The plot's disruption—saving the King's life!—
You cannot possibly mean this?— Oh mercy!

    SFOR. I mean it, if you do.

    LAURA. Do what!— Oh, sir!

Answer me!—do not hold me in swinging chains,
With the flames rising!—burn me up at once
In your conclusion!

    SFOR. (*fiercely*) Name all the accomplices,
Or your child dies! (*going*)

    LAURA. (*madly*) No—no—I will do anything!
A moment, I beseech you! Say to the King,
That as my life should pay the penalty
Of this my obstinate silence, I am ready
To lay it down—freely to cast it down—
Humbly and thankfully—but spare my child!

    SFOR. In vain. You have heard the alternative. [*going* (R.)

    LAURA. (*hoarsely*) Oh wolf!
Oh, worse than wolf——let me consider it.

    SFOR. (*returning*) Lead her back to the dungeon, some
    few minutes.

[*Laura is led back by Guards, and the dungeon door is closed.* [comes forth.

SFOR. (*half aside*) She may think differently when she (*To Guards*) Bring out the Jew.

[*Exeunt two Guards to the 3rd dungeon* (L.)

SFOR. (*half aside*) Not often do we fail
To wrench, or spin their secrets from these rebels.

Enter SKURDENKA, *with Guards, from dungeon* (L.)

SFOR. Now, Jew!

SKUR. Now, poisoner!

SFOR. So. (*turning aside his head*)

SKUR. I smelt the drug.

SFOR. Tut!

SKUR. Do you not believe me?

SFOR. You could not.

SKUR. Then there *was* some inodorous poison there?
I drank no water. 'Tis my will to die
In my right senses.

SFOR. (*to Guard*) Take him back to his dungeon!
Stay! (*aside*) There's no knowing. (*aloud*) Michael Skurdenka!
In one word, do you wish to save your life?

SKUR. To *keep* my life, I wish. I do not like
The word " save," for it smacks of some foul service.

SFOR. (*aside*) The only chance were now to flay his pride.
(*aloud*) I simply asked you to betray your friends,
Who join'd in this conspiracy to murder
A virtuous King. Do you call that a foul service?

SKUR. (*astonished*) Beyond all doubt!
SFOR. If so, 'twill suit thee well,
Thou son and heir of an accursed race!
SKUR. What is thy race? Italian: a great race!
The greater villain thou who canst betray
Thy country. How far higher were thy state,
Wert thou, like me, a prisoner in the cause
Of liberty; yet more—a victim now—
For other lands than mine. Thou wear'st a sword,
But hast no honest soldier's patriot heart,
Like his, who in yon dungeon's midnight hell,
With poison'd nerves, pour'd forth a prayer to God,
For Hungary!—midst pausing sighs—while oft
His sinking voice, in faint delirium, raised
A battle-cry 'neath Buda's frosty towers! [wealth,
SFOR. While thou, bethought'st thee of the hoarded
From Christians filched—the widow's—orphan's tears—
Thy bearded Rabbi father lost in Warsaw! [dead!
SKUR. (*with dignity*) Slander the soul of the majestic
What manner of man is this! That Rabbi gave—
As did my family—root, stem, and branch—
All they possess'd on earth—gold, jewels, raiment—
Sold off a costly share our house long held
In the salt mines of the Carpathian mountains,
To aid the desperate fights of Grochow—Praga—
On the high road to Warsaw. He completed
Their gifts—my Rabbi father at their head—
By laying down, in death, his sacred beard
Begrimed with dust and blood of Russian serfs,
At Ostrolenka! There my Hebrew sire

Died like a man—as thou shalt never die,
Earth-damn'd and heaven-damn'd slave!
   SFOR. (*aside*) He warms apace.
(*aloud*) Many a Polish Jew sold arms and food
To Russia: These were patriots!
   SKUR. No—villains!
Gentiles who sold their country—dogs like thee!
   (*Moves towards the door of Laura's dungeon*).
   SFOR. (*aside*) Something comes now.
   SKUR. Thou brave-soul'd, tortured lady!—
Worthy the history of those other lands—
The Pole's, the Magyar's—when with patriot fire,
Women of all ranks, with their children, worked
I' the trenches!—beautiful young maidens stood
On ball-rent bastions, or in the foremost ranks
Defended their dear country—(Warsaw's glory
Ne'er topp'd that hour)—thou brave Italian lady!
As thou respects't thy husband and thyself,
Make *no* terms with this caitiff!
   SFOR. (*loudly*) Jew, beware!
   (SKURDENKA *turns fiercely towards* SFORGLIA).
   SKUR. Speak's thou of widow's and of orphan's tears!
Heard I not through my dungeon's grated door,
How thou didst threat to take an infant's life,
Unless its mother would betray the men
Who by its father in worst peril stood?
Serpent!—she now is sitting on the ground,
Balancing maddening loads upon her brain!
Go to her!—comfort her!—release her child,
And take it to her! So shalt thou understand
A Jew hath taught thee Christianity!

SFOR. (*to Guards*) Gag this hot maniac!.... No!—
    there's something better.
Bring back the Hungarian!
    (*Exeunt Guards into the dungeon of* BATTHYMAROS.)
(*To* SKURDENKA *indirectly*) We can goad a bull
To its last stall!
    SKUR. Thy victims to the shambles.
A King can do no butchery. (*advancing*)
    (*At a signal from* SFORGLIA *the Guards drag him back*).

Re-enter Guards, leading BATTHYMAROS *slowly from his
    dungeon, under the influence of belladonna.*
    SFOR. Hungarian prisoner!
    BATT. (*shaking his head, with half-closed eyes*) I do not
        understand men's purposes.
    SFOR. Know this!
You are order'd for immediate execution.
    BATT. (*mildly turning to go*) Sir, I am ready.
    SFOR. But the King empowers me
To spare your life.   [DENKA.
    BATT. I thank his Majesty. (*then turning to* SKUR-
I may say as much, with honour—don't you think so?
    (*pressing his hand over his forehead*)
And yet, I feel as if it came too late.
    SFOR. Arouse your faculties—and understand
There are conditions. Name all accomplices
In the late plot.
    BATT. Ah! do I understand?—
No, sir—no, sir—I do not.
    SFOR. Think an instant.

SCENE IV.] LAURA DIBALZO. 73

BATT. (*after looking sadly at* SKURDENKA, *and then vacantly in the air*).
I know this is a moment of my life
I should be most myself—and I am nothing—
A soldier melted to a sword's flat shade—
Sunk down to nought, yet ever sinking still—
All but a throbbing something in my heart
Which says I *was* a man;—and I will die
Without disgracing that bright memory
(*humbly*) With this poor sheath! (*drops his arms*).

SFOR. (*to* SKURDENKA) One chance remains for thee,
By intercession of the Cardinal.
Wilt thou become a convert to our Church?

SKUR. After your model?—or the King's?

SFOR. Enough.
One chance is profferr'd now to both of you.
The first who speaks, doth win it. Thou—Skurdenka!
Wilt thou do execution—shoot the Hungarian—
Wearing the Cap of Liberty, the while?
Hungarian!—wilt thou hang the Polish Jew?
Who answers first? Quick!

[SKURDENKA *advances towards* BATTHYMAROS *and* BATTHYMAROS *feebly towards* SKURDENKA: *the two men, with noble tears, embrace each other; then turn with dignity, and smile at* SFORGLIA.

SFOR. (*biting the fingers of his left hand*) Lead them to instant death!

[*Exeunt* (L. 2nd E.)

SCENE V.—[1st *Entrance*].

Front of the King's private Oratory. Door (U.C.)

Enter the KING *and* SAN-VOLPE (U.C.)

KING. That's well—that's good: go on, thou holy man.
SAN-VOL. And thus they have dug a pit-fall for themselves.
KING. You sniff'd this during a penitent confession
Of one i' the secret?
SAN-VOL. (*closing his eyes*) Oh, no!
KING. Afterwards? [God.
SAN-VOL. We are bound to serve our King, as well as
KING. That's very true.
   Enter SFORGLIA (R.)
    We have o'er-topped you, sir,
In your high duties. We have found the den
Prepared by traitors for their friends to lurk
In fatal safety. Through your iron-clad hands,
Like falcons ill-secured they sought free life,
Cleaving the darkness with their scornful wings.
Be prompt for your own redemption. With strong guard
Attend us here to-night: ourself would go
To enjoy their death-blank faces. [*Exit* SFORGLIA.

(*to* SAN-VOLPE) Heaven directs us,
Protects and comforts us each step we take,
And blesses us in everything we do.
(*pausing*) Except in dealing with Dibalzo's wife.
That woman is in league . . . . (*breathless with rage*).
  SAN-VOL. With whom, my Lord?
    (*The King stamps upon the ground.*)
  KING. With Satan!—not the figurative Satan—
Nor as in missals, poems, tapestries, nightmares,
Painted, and sung, and stitch'd, and brimstone-boil'd—
But the embodied Emperor of Hell,
To whom the adulteress Laura is espoused!
Yes, Satan! or she could not thus have braved
Maternal tortures—thus her head up-held,
And 'gainst Our Church and godly Crown rebell'd.
                             [*Exeunt.*

END OF THE FOURTH ACT.

ACT V.

SCENE I.—[4th Entrance.]

Dilapidated ornamental Fountain in the grove of a ruined Villa. Mutilated statues of forms once beautiful (one in especial, symbolizing Italy) with a Sea Monster in the centre, wearing a grotesque crown. Lofty broken rocks at the back. Moon slowly rising. Deep shadows. Sound of falling waters.

RIVEROLA *seen descending a secret zig-zag pathway of the rocks. He pauses; then beckons off* (L.) *and* GUARINI, DIBALZO, *and two Nobles follow him down the rocks.*

RIVE. Here—as you know, I long have pre-arranged,
In case of need—you may secrete yourselves.
Beneath yon marble ruin is a chamber,
For water built, now furnish'd with dry weeds.
I've placed provisions there.
    DIBAL. My lord, we thank you. (*to Nobles*) Now 'twere best return,
Lest that your absence bring you in suspicion.

RIVE. Can we do ought more yet?
1st NOBLE (*going* L.) Aye, each for himself.
To all our friends, as now, I say the same.
I shall away to England. These are times
When men should use their heads if they would keep them,
Nor leave their gold too near the smelter's fire.
That's my advice—so gentlemen, farewell! [*Exit* (L.)
RIVE. A man whose country in his coffer lies!
GUAR. Too much prosperity damages the heart,
Though the heart knows it not. Hold him excused.
2nd NOBLE. He cannot pass the frontier?
RIVE. If he reach it.
GUAR. (*to* RIVEROLA *and* NOBLE) Return to the city,
    I entreat you.   [*taking* RIVEROLA *by the arm.*
RIVE. (*going*) We will find means to visit you anon.
GUAR. I pray you go!
DIBAL. *A Dio*, my lords!
RIVE. *Addio!* (*they embrace*)

[*Exeunt* RIVEROLA *and* NOBLE (R. 2nd E.)

DIBAL. (*after a pause*) Here then, Guarini, we are
    brought to bay,
With night-hounds round us, and our ardent hopes
And great designs, exchanged for narrowing thoughts,
And secret means to hold the breath of life,—
Our Country sacrificed to scrupulous saws
About the taking of a tyrant's life!
Thy meditations, and thine adverse words
Have ruined all!
GUAR. This is not generous.

DIBAL. No, but 'tis just. Thy moral arguments—
Good in the mouth of a safe Englishman,
But despots' food, and suicide in us—
Delayed my movements—paralysed the blow
Just as the arm was raised.

GUAR. 'Tis a sad time
For these reproaches. I spoke what I thought,
And for the best, and I am at your side
To stand or fall with you.

DIBAL. Why do we fall?
Because we did not in good season rise,
And act upon conviction. Your ohs, and ahs,
And English moral shakings of the head,
Learnt on your visits to that envied land,
Are they for one side only?—for the side
Of wholesale murders, and against the men
Who'd quell one single pest—and stamp it out?
Tell it to the moon—there it may pass for sense,
Tell't to the great Star-banner'd Continent,
Or in free Britain, where the people's eyes
Can give no reason to imagine facts
Which are our daily curse, or cause to feel them;
But we who are i'the middle of this hell,
Are the best judges of our own sensations!

GUAR. My brother!—nay, be patient.

DIBAL. Do you forget
I have a wife and child?—and where are they?

GUAR. Laura escaped before us, and your friend
The Jailer, has fled with her—or, perchance,
The penitent Ilario.

SCENE I.]   LAURA DIBALZO.   79

 DIBAL. Possibly—
But where?—where—where? (*he weeps*)
 GUAR. (*going*) I'll forth in search of them.
 DIBAL. (*catching him in his arms*) Forgive my incoherent, passionate grief!
'Tis fed from many sources, which produce
A uniform confusion. For some hours—
Perhaps all night, I pray remain you here;
I must seek tidings, nay, in sooth I *must*—
This hideous quietude will drive me mad—
Impassive to the storm that dins within me:
I will return forthwith.
   (*Going, he staggers from exhaustion.*)
 GUAR. Stay here, Dibalzo,
And rest awhile. A little sleep will give you
A better ground for effort, as for hope.
 DIBAL. (*sinking down*) Do you think so? O, Laura!
O, my child!
  (*The moon passes behind clouds.* DIBALZO *sleeps.*)
   [GUARINI *walks up, and contemplates the broken
    statuary of the Fountain; then comes down.*

 GUAR. When will the struggles of Humanity—
The millions of all nations, times, and creeds,
Against the monomaniac despots, cease,
And man discover life's best ordered scheme?
'Tis not the question of how many deaths,
Through insurrections, exiles, dungeons, scaffolds,
Nor e'en the fall of many an untrain'd mass,
Like sheep by liveried butchers' skilful hands,

Be requisite to gain earth's one grand right;—
Life, in the aggregate, is a sacrifice,
From whose high altars revelations flow
In crimson streams. Sometimes through broken hearts
New systems of man's loftier culture rise,
Nourish'd by all these graves, and by the spirit—
The surging murmur of the popular soul—
That ever sings above them. Oh, I hear thee!
I long have heard—and hear thee clearer now—
Perhaps for the last time. Our course is run;
In some things noble, both in thought and deed,
In others mixed—shot with keen glancing doubts,
And inward whisperings of the tree of life—
The heart's red secrets—only known to God.

(DIBALZO *moans in his sleep.*)

Yet individual lives, not sacred held,
Or more than water when compared with kings,
Are sacred yet to memory, when given
Pure offerings tow'rds a great and general good.
The blood of the true patriot is a gift
Which heaven cherishes; in some other form,
Such as his best hopes dreamt, it seeks the light,
Inspires the root, the branch of future years,
Nor unrewarded lost within the flower.

(*Walks up towards the fountain, and seats himself.*)

Then why lament discomfitures, and deaths,
Which, in the common round of waste, are few?
How many thousand lives are lost at sea
Each year, in reefing sails, or by the chance

Of some less cause? Man must accept the law
Of nature wisely, but the social law
Compel to wisdom by conformity
With nature. Yet, each individual life
Should be held sacred (else no common path
Were safe from murder)—not a *subject's* life,
When danger threats one jewel of a crown !
Thy life, Dibalzo—all our lives—as many
As the occasion needs—what is't to one
That grimly sits, reigning for history !
      (DIBALZO *awakes, and rises hastily.*)
  DIBAL. Why did you let me sleep?—have I slept long?
I must away some tidings to obtain
Of Laura, and my child. Which way's the best?
Know you this place?
  GUAR. I know it well, and will direct your steps.
  DIBAL. I will return anon.
  GUAR. Take close disguise.
     [*They ascend the zig-zag path through the rocks,*
      and disappear at the top. The moon emerges
      from clouds. Sound of falling waters.

Enter KING, SFORGLIA, *and a number of Guards.* (R.)

  KING. Here glooms the den! a squarrose spot where
Oft paint and poetize, but where no hunters   [dolts
E'er track'd a game like ours. (*seats himself*)
     (SFORGLIA *directs two Guards with drawn*
      swords to descend into the cavern).
  KING. Now will their eyes
Outshine the steel that's pointed at their breasts !

(*Guards re-ascend, bringing up two baskets
of provisions*).

SFOR. Not yet arrived.

KING. (*laughing*) A very different food
Will soon be in their throats. Search well around,
Perchance you'll meet them coming.

[*Exeunt* SFORGLIA *and several Guards* (L),
and all the other Guards (R).

KING. Plunder blinds
A soldier's eyes to all else. (*rising*) Papers! books—
Letters—hand-writing! Ha! the fatal pen!
But what I find I'll keep close—specially
From doom'd ones. *Qui nescit dissimulare,
Nescit regnare.* These bush-berries smell
Of treason as of poison. Letters—scraps——

[*The* KING, *pushing brambles aside, descends
into the cavern. Sound of falling waters,
and cry of night-birds.* GUARINI *appears
at the top of the rocks, and descends. He
pauses thoughtfully.*

GUAR. His heart, I fear, will show through all disguise,
As would a ruby in a monk's hood set.

(*Advances towards the sculptures over
the cavern*).

GUAR. The struggles of mankind can never prove
Victorious o'er earth's despots, till the time
When soldiers will be citizens—not tools—
And a wise people use their wealth aright.
Yet meanwhile I have waited for the dawn

Of man's fair day too long, and I am weary,—
Waited, and planned, with beating brain to see,
First of all hopes, this stony monster fall,
And beautiful Italia rise once more
In just proportions. I grow sick of time—
And almost court its close.

KING. (*stepping out of the cavern with his sword drawn*)
That hour is come!—Ha! guards! my guards!
(*wildly on both sides*) Traitors! guards! guards!
    GUAR. (*drawing*) We are alone! RINI.)
    KING. (*choking*) Guards! traitors! (*rushing at* GUA-

    (GUARINI *strikes the sword out of the
        King's hand.*

    GUAR. Take up thy sword—and make thy peace with
        Heaven!
    KING. (*snatching up his sword*) Ha! would you dare?
    GUAR. What?
    KING. Kill me?
    GUAR. Instantly!
    KING. (*stamping upon the ground*) Guards! traitors!
    GUAR. Man to man! Defend your life!
It is as surely lost as is your soul! (*advancing*)
    KING. (*retreating*) I know you, Count Guarini!
    GUAR. (*still advancing*) Know me better!

    (*Wounding the* KING, *who leans upon
        his sword*).

    KING. (*in dismay*) Hold! hold your hand a moment—
        something to say!
I promise to release your sister!

GUAR. Friends? [now—
KING. I swear it!—all your friends,—child,—'prison'd Accomplices—all, all—(*faintly*) my Guards!
GUAR. (*sternly, with his sword pointing at* SALOMBA'S *breast*) And liberate all political prisoners, In dungeons chained?
KING. Yes—Count Guarini—yes!
GUAR. Swear also to vacate the throne of Naples?
KING. (*staggering back*) Throne! throne!—resign my throne?
GUAR. Or take thy death! [thee!
KING. My crown I hold, and death—death give to Oh, I will kill—rend, rend thee into atoms!

> [*The* KING *rushes wildly upon* GUARINI, *who parrying his thrusts, casts him to the ground, and sets one foot upon him.*
>
> SFORGLIA *and Guards rush in* (L.). *Other Guards* (R.). SFORGLIA *and two Guards seize* GUARINI *from behind.* GUARINI *throws down his sword.* SFORGLIA *comes to the front and takes up the sword*).

GUAR. Had you obtained it from me face to face, It had become you better.
SFOR. (*tremblingly anxious*) Gracious King?

> [*Exeunt* (R.). *The* KING *supported,* GUARINI *guarded.*

SCENE II.—[2nd Entrance.]

Street in Naples. Shouts of rabble outside. Voices crying "Drag him along"! "Drag him along"!

Enter Guards with DIBALZO *in chains* (L), *followed by Lazzaroni, Peasants, Sailors, and Rabble.* STRONG'ITH'ARM *appears at an open window.*)

Voices. Drag him along! drag him along!

1st. LAZZ. Let us see him shot, the impious traitor!

2nd LAZZ. Or beheaded, or hung,—or both!

1st PEASANT. Or rather crushed by the great stone—that's the best death to see!

Voices. So it is! so it is!

1st SAILOR. There's a fine American sloop in the bay. Woulds't not ha' liked to get aboard of her, and sail away to the States, where they've got no king?

DIBAL. (*scornfully*) They are much better without one—especially such a tyrant as slaves like you worship.

1st. PEASANT. (*crossing himself in dismay*) Hear him blaspheme our most religious King! This man would dispute and deny a miracle!

2nd PEASANT. The best we ever saw, would he!

(*Shouts outside, answered by shouts from those in the street*).

STRONG'ITH'ARM. (*from a window*) Peace, brutal mob! Respect the silent death-march of the men who sought to raise your foreheads from the dust!

(*Yells and a shower of stones at the window*).

Voices. (*in the street*) Yes, you are beasts!—idiots!—these men were patriots!—but an Insurrection will soon . . . . .

(*General confusion*).

Voices. (*from a parapet*) Valiente! animo!

Voices. (*in the street*) A Spanish refugiado!

Voices. (*from the parapet*) Yes—Spain has also had her patriot martyrs.

(*Yells and stones thrown at the parapet*).

A Voice. Los Mexicanos y otros, tambien!

(*Yells and mockeries*).

Voices. Les Français!—Die Deutschen!

(*Redoubled showers of missiles*).

1st PEASANT. Here comes another of the heretic traitors!

Enter SFORGLIA *and Guards* (L.) *with* GUARINI *in chains.*

1st LAZZ. (*to* GUARINI) You too, Signor assassin, and high-treason villain! We shall all rejoice to see you put under the great stone!

(GUARINI *looks at him with composure*).

1st SAILOR (*to* GUARINI). You also would have been glad to slip off safe to England, or America, or Cape Fly-away; but we've got you lash'd fast in the jail-rigging (*tapping the chains*).

1st PEASANT (*to* GUARINI). Cross swords with our anointed Sovereign!—you who should lick the dust before the blessed feet of pious Salomba's Majesty!

A PRIEST (*to* GUARINI). O, thou accursed one!

Voices. To the great stone!

1st LAZZ. The executioners should pluck out their beards by the roots, and their finger nails too, as was done to some rebels the other day at the Vicaria; and they should be laid chained together on the dungeon floor, to be gnawed by the rats till they went mad!—No new thing for such as these.

Voices. The stone! to the great stone!

1st PEASANT. Cowards, dastardly cowards both of you!

DIBAL. The scribbler's verbiage! It is the people's cowardice
That plants the poniard in the patriot's hand,
Which else had led them forward with a sword!

(GUARINI *places one hand on* DIBALZO'S *shoulder to pacify him.* SFORGLIA *advances with a menacing air.*

Voices. Well said! we like all this! ha! ha! ha! There's some strong and holy life here, before death and the devil, after all! Down with all Insurrectionists!

SFOR. (*to Guards*) Forward with the prisoners!

[*Exeunt* (R.)

SCENE III.—[4th Entrance.]

Street in Naples, with ornamental wall (U. C.), *and the Palace in the distance, (as in* ACT 1, SC. 1). *Sky dark, with gloomy red clouds. Massive wooden shears are visible beyond the top of the wall, with lifting tackle attached. A bell tolls; and then a flourish of trumpets is heard.*

Enter KING *and* SAN-VOLPE (L. 1st E.) *with attendants.*

KING. Much hurt?—not I—we are too good a king;
(*aside*) But Sforglia shall pay dear for that, ere long:
I'll teach my blood-hound's snout a broader scent.
　SAN-VOL. Dibalzo safe once more, Guarini chained,
The rest will follow.
　KING. This conspiracy
Is wider spread than we at first had thought:
Nobles and gentlemen of different States,
Nay, some about the Court are mixed in it—
Men of large wealth—and several citizens,
Artists, and men of letters.
　SAN-VOL. Students also,
I fear.
　KING. No doubt—a most ungodly set.
But we'll probe deep the inmost nerves of sense,

SCENE III.] LAURA DIBALZO.

Till name on name spouts from the affrighted heart,
Or crush their secrets in them.
  SAN-VOL. I believe
Your Majesty will find no other means.
Thrice, in my holy office, have I sought
To bring the woman to due penitence,
And full communion—but in vain.
  KING. I know;— (*looking off* L.)
Yet we will have her secrets. See, she comes!
Sforglia hath orders from me how to act.
(*to* SAN-VOLPE, *interrogatively*)
Something miraculous may come of this?
                              [*Exeunt* (R. U.E.)

Enter LAURA, *wildly, followed by* SFÓRGLIA *and Guards*
                              (L. 1st E.)

  LAURA. Where is the King? where is the King?—
    you told me
He came this way!—my child—what, kill my child!
Threaten to smother—to suffocate by law—
An infant of six years!
  SFOR. Name *all* the accomplices——   [swear.
  LAURA. My child!—my child! I know them not, I
  SFOR. Those then, you *do* know. You have been
    informed,
We have your husband and your brother safe.
  LAURA. Ha! is that true? I did not hear!—is't true?
  SFOR. They will be léd to instant execution,
If they, like you, reject the King's demand.
But your child dies the first.

LAURA (*holding her head*). 'Tis not heaven's will—
SFOR. But the King's will.
LAURA. That comes from another place—
You would not .... oh, forbear!

Enter GUARINI *in chains, guarded* (L.)

LAURA (*rushing towards him*). Guarini!—they—
My child—Edita——
GUAR. (*solemnly*) Sister, be comforted.
LAURA. What would you say?
GUAR. I heard it whispered, as they brought me here,
Their harsh devices had o'er-wrought the aim,
And Christ had ta'en his own. Your child is dead!
LAURA (*falling upon her knees; then looking up*).
I thank thee, Christ—and I am comforted—
Sure friend in life's profoundest misery!
GUAR. 'Twas not the mercy that Salomba planned.

Enter a Messenger (L.) *who places a paper in* SFORGLIA'S
hand, and retires to the rear.

SFOR. (*after looking over the paper*) Do you know
  this writing, Madam?
LAURA. I can see nothing—do not speak to me.
SFOR. The time is short.
GUAR. Dear sister, yet be strong;
It will soon be over.
LAURA. (*to* SFORGLIA) What did you ask me, sir?
SFOR. (*handing the paper*) Do you know this writing?
LAURA. (*glancing at it*) No!

SFOR. (*pointedly*) The signature! (*she hesitates*)
GUAR. Answer him, Laura.
LAURA. But you do not.... (*she stops*)
GUAR. Yes—I set my foot upon His Majesty,—
I know it matters not.
LAURA. (*to* SFORGLIA) My husband's, sir.

(SFORGLIA *takes the paper from her.*)

May I not see what's written?
SFOR. (*to* GUARINI) 'Tis for you.

> [LAURA *stands apart in her distress, while*
> SFORGLIA *takes* GUARINI *confidentially aside.*

SFOR. In my harsh duties I have dealt by you
With little courtesy; but private malice
Against you, I have none. Now look you here.
(*showing the paper*) But first look yonder!

> [*A huge broad and flat stone is slowly hoisted to
> the upper part of the shears, and remains fixed.*

(*Voices and noise outside among advancing crowds.*)

SFOR. 'Tis understood your earnest voice opposed
Our King's assassination. Why should you—
A gentleman of birth and studious thought,
In honour held by all, be sacrificed
To madmen; doubly traitors—first to the King,
Next to their friends? Just read this paper, sir.
GUAR. (*takes the paper and reads, half aside*) "I hereby solemnly offer to divulge the names of all those implicated in the late plot,—from the Signor Guarini, and our

patrician friends, down to the lowest hireling, on condition that His Majesty will generously and mercifully spare my life, so justly forfeited to the laws, both human and divine. Signed in presence of these attesting witnesses,

CLAUDIO DIBALZO."

[GUARINI *starts slightly, then fixes his eyes upon the signature.*

SFOR. (*still aside to him*) You thought it simply treason
—not this treachery ?
Like to the man, Ilario, so the master!
Well sir, the King rejects such evidence,
And this forgiving favour proffers you.
Promote the arrest of all accomplices,
And you are free. (*aloud*) Here is the royal pardon!

[*Places a parchment with large seal in* GUARINI'S *hand.* LAURA *hurries forward.*

LAURA. My brother pardon'd!—oh, 'tis very right—
His views were different—
GUAR. (*calmly returning the first paper*) 'Tis a forgery!
SFOR. (*with affected astonishment*) His wife avowed the signature!
GUAR. Her sight
Dazed through the scalding outlets of her grief:
It is not his. But say, it were?
SFOR. What then?

(GUARINI *quietly throws down the King's pardon.*)

You have thrown away your life!
LAURA. Alas! my brother!

GUAR. A man has only one life on the earth,
And therefore should pick well his heavenward way,
Having no second chance. Oh Italy!
You can afford to lose a faithful son,
Many so true remain. I felt it honour
To live for you, and now the higher honour
To die for you.

(*Sound of chains without.*)

LAURA. My husband!—yes, tis he. O cruel chains!

Enter DIBALZO *in chains, guarded* (L.); *a crowd, chiefly of women, follow.*

DIBAL. Laura!

[LAURA *rushes into* DIBALZO'S *arms. They are separated at a sign from* SFORGLIA.

LAURA (*extending her arms towards* DIBALZO). Do you know of Edith's death?

DIBAL. (*restraining his emotion*) Yes—Laura—yes – Do not unman me. We shall meet her soon.

LAURA (*to* SFORGLIA *with calm pathos*). When shall we die?

SFOR. 'Tis order'd.

GUAR. (*coldly*) What do we wait for?

SFOR. His Majesty's signal from the Palace tower,
Where he will stand to see two traitors crushed.

DIBAL. By yonder stone?

SFOR. Aye, by the stone.

LAURA (*shuddering*) Oh God! (*imploringly to* SFORGLIA) Not by that frightful death!

DIBAL. Plead not, my wife;
'Tis better than the torture you have suffer'd
In thoughts of me, and Edita—slowly murdered—
LAURA. By royal hands that now destroy you both!
DIBAL. (*to* LAURA) This is the king we were too nice
  to kill!—
You would do it now?
  LAURA (*clasping her hands*). Were he a hundred kings!
  GUAR. Be patient, sister; let us compose our spirits.
  LAURA. But the appalling stone!
  GUAR. (*deliberately*) I object to that.
  SFOR. (*malignantly*) 'Tis like you do. (*suppressing a
   brutal laugh*)
  GUAR. But not for the poor reason in your mind.
  SFOR. What other then?
  GUAR. Because if man be made
In the image of God, I should prefer to die
In that august resemblance.

    Enter SAN-VOLPE (R. U.E.)

SAN-VOL. But the arch-fiend
Transfigured you to rebels, and 'tis good
That forms so vile were changed.
  SFOR. The signal's made! (*walks up a few paces*)
  LAURA (*after a struggle*). You cannot crush their souls!
  SAN-VOL. (*darkly*) We know not that.
  GUAR. *I* know it!
  SFOR. Bring them away!
  GUAR. Shades of the noble dead, we follow ye!
   (*Walks up in advance of the Guards.*)

DIBAL. (*with upraised hand*) Cyro Menotti! Andryane!
  Miglio!
Ruffini! noble brothers Bandiera!
Shades of Vocchieri! Romeo! Andreoli!
Shades from three thousand scaffolds of Radetzski,
All hail! we come to your embracing arms!
  GUAR. Oh, not in vain they suffer'd—nor shall we:
The death of many a martyr aids the cause
More than his life could do.   We are content.
My sister—and my brother—one embrace!
  (*They embrace, then walk to the back.*)
  DIBAL. (*embracing* LAURA *closely*) My wife—Laura—
  my wife—
(LAURA *is unable to speak. Weeping among the crowd*).
  DIBAL. Be firm against their last temptations—
Promise me!
  LAURA. Yes—Yes—
  DIBAL. Laura!— (*both are overcome*)
  GUAR. (*coming down to* LAURA) Look on us, well—
  two men prepared to die!
Sister, do honour to yourself, and us.
Be steadfast—clear—bright-eyed as adamant:
Be steel—be fire lock'd up in flint—be cold
With power—and let thy spirit petrify
Each nerve for this last moment!   So, we bless you!
  [GUARINI *and* DIBALZO *walk up with an erect
  bearing, and take their station between the
  Guards at the back* (*near* R. U.E.). *Smothered
  sobs heard among the crowd.*

DIBAL. (*gazing at* LAURA) Thou holy image 'midst these heathen rites!

[*A signal bell is struck*—LAURA, *shuddering all over, covers her head with her hands.*]

GUAR. (*joining hands with* DIBALZO) Our earthly pilgrimage had many halts;
A moment's flight, and we are safe—in heaven!

[*Exeunt* GUARINI *and* DIBALZO, *with Guards* (R.U.E.)

The Scene darkens. Distant flashes of lightning.

[*Enter Populace, Lazzaroni, Peasants, Insurrectionists, Sailors, etc.,* (L. 2nd & U.E.) *They eagerly climb halfway up the wall, to see the execution. Several lean over the top of the wall, all faces being turned in the direction of the King's Palace.* SAN-VOLPE *stands watchfully aside;* SFORGLIA *in front with* LAURA.]

LAURA (*raising her head wildly*). Are they gone? will they pause awhile on the way?
Will they return for an instant?—why are you here?

SFOR. To offer the last chance those lunatics told you
Not to accept.

LAURA. My life?—what is that worth?
Hark! hark! (*listening with a frantic air*)

SFOR. No—no—you are mistaken. 'Tis not
The moment of their death. That rests with *you*.

LAURA. With *me?*

SFOR. Their deaths, or else their lives.

LAURA (*imploringly*). Oh, sir,
Have you a human heart! this is too cruel.

SFOR. Not so. Their lives, I say, are in your hands.
LAURA. How?
SFOR. Name at once all the conspirators—
Your brother and your husband will be spared.
LAURA (*catching at the thought*). Is't true?
(*then staggered*) Is this really true?
SFOR. By the King's word.
LAURA (*incredulously*). Oh, we're all doomed to die—
    I know it well.
If I should do this thing, how could I meet
My husband face to face in the other world?
SFOR. You refuse then?
LAURA. I——I——
SFOR. Stop!—only one word—one word.
"Yes"—you accept the terms, "No"—and at once
The stone descends!   (*signal bell is struck again.*)
They're placed beneath it now!
LAURA (*frantically*). Now, do you say! now, now
    beneath the stone?
Hark! it has fallen! hark! it falls! falls! falls!
Did I not hear it?—but I hear it still!
Oh, 'tis my throbbing brain! This is too much—
Too much for nature. Stay the falling stone!
I will say anything to save them!—stop!
Make signal! Is it only yes, or no?
Immortal souls hang on a syllable!
Truth, honour, woman's weakness, falsehood, firmness,
My husband's last injunction—and my brother's—
    SFOR. Both suicides through you unless you save them!
    LAURA. A true wife trusted with the last extremes,

Must not be false when this last .... stay the signal!
A moment! yet a moment!—but one moment—
In case I lose my senses—as I *shall* do—

   (*She rushes to and fro.*)

I see it in the air, and the mad sky,
Now full of fiery faces, and the shadows
Of constant stones descending!—my brain's stunn'd
With crushing sounds!—I shall be raving soon—
My throat is choked with blood! I must go mad—
And then I might consent—so God assist me
To stand up in my grave-clothes, and say "No!"

  [LAURA *stands up erectly as she utters the last words. A stroke on the bell is heard. She crouches and reels. The great stone descends with a dull vibrating sound.*—LAURA *utters a cry. A distant shout is heard. She falls dead.* SFORGLIA *and* SAN-VOLPE *hurry to her, and exchange signs of her death.*

  [*Populace, &c., leap down from the wall. Shouts of an Insurrection—shots are fired, poniards and knives gleam on all sides—*SFORGLIA *and* SAN-VOLPE *are stabbed by many hands, and a flash of lightning strikes the King's Palace as the curtain descends.*

www.ingramcontent.com/pod-product-compliance
Lightning Source LLC
Chambersburg PA
CBHW030408170426
43202CB00010B/1536